IN STRICTEST CONFIDENCE

Also by Craig Revel Horwood:

All Balls and Glitter

Tales from the Dance Floor

IN STRICTEST CONFIDENCE

CRAIG REVEL HORWOOD

with Alison Maloney

Michael O'Mara Books Limited

This revised and updated paperback edition first published in 2019

First published in hardback in Great Britain in 2018 by
Michael O'Mara Books Limited
9 Lion Yard
Tremadoc Road
London SW4 7NQ

A CIP catalogue record for this book is available from the British Library.

Papers used by Michael O'Mara Books Limited are natural, recyclable
products made from wood grown in sustainable forests. The manufacturing
processes conform to the environmental regulations of the country of origin.

ISBN: 978-1-78929-159-9 in paperback print format
ISBN: 978-1-78929-035-6 in ebook format
ISBN: 978-1-78929-060-8 in audiobook format

1 2 3 4 5 6 7 8 9 10

www.mombooks.com

Designed and typeset by Barbara Ward

Printed and bound by CPI Group (UK) Ltd, Croydon, CR0 4YY

Contents

Prologue

I n the summer of 2018, I came face-to-face with myself on the dance floor of the legendary Tower Ballroom in Blackpool. The occasion was the unveiling of my waxwork, which was destined for the town's Madame Tussauds, and it has to be one of the most bizarre moments of my life. The life-sized effigy, lovingly crafted by the Tussauds' amazing team, was so realistic that when I was standing next to it my own mum had trouble telling us apart. It was unnerving to see me the way that the rest of the world did, complete with every grey hair, wrinkle, skin blemish and freckle. At the age of 53 I had finally found myself – literally.

Joking aside, the incredible honour of being immortalized in wax at Madame Tussauds left me in a reflective mood. Who would have believed this boy from Ballarat would one day stand alongside the most legendary names in show business, sport and global politics at the world-famous waxwork attraction? How had that chubby kid who dreamed of dancing on the West End stage ended up here?

Since I last put pen to paper, for *Tales from the Dance Floor*, my life has taken many twists and turns and, of course, the odd plié. I have celebrated my half-century – in my customary lavish style – and moved to a country pile. I have loved and lost, and loved again. I have starred in a West End show in drag and made my film debut in equally outrageous get-up. I have discovered my ancestry, by appearing on *Who Do You Think You Are?*, and I have, sadly, lost my father.

Throughout it all, *Strictly Come Dancing* has remained a constant in my life. We witnessed the triumphs of the most amazing finals ever and the sad departure of key players, including Len Goodman and Bruce Forsyth, but the show still goes from strength to strength, I'm happy to say.

As readers of my first two books will know, dance has been my world, and the reason I have had such a varied and enjoyable career so far. So join me, once again, for a twirl around the dance floor of my life.

CHAPTER 1

A Country Squire

As the 2014 *Strictly* season got going, I was experiencing the gruelling process of moving house. Since coming to the UK thirty years ago, I had lived in a listed two-up two-down in Camden Town. The London street I lived in has a line of pretty pastel facades and, to no one's surprise, my place was a gorgeous shade of pink. I loved the history of the house, and to have something I could call my own was beyond fabulous. Over the years I lived there, I made a close-knit group of friends that I still spend time with today. It was so special having them live so close. They could just pop in anytime. These friends were, and still are, my village of support; the fact that they were so accessible was the main reason that I stayed in my little London home for so many years.

In the early days, Camden was a fairly rough area that attracted more than its fair share of unsavoury characters, which is possibly why it was affordable to me at the time. But things that I would normally take in my stride were starting to wear me down in my advancing years. Vagrants were always urinating on my doorstep. I even interrupted one distinguished gentleman as he relieved himself. I was wearing my Prada shoes at the time, and they didn't fare well with what seemed like ten pints of lager splashed across them. Another very bleak night, a homeless fellow actually defecated in the same spot – not on my Prada shoes, thank God, but he left a nice steaming message on my welcome mat! To my horror, I caught that little gem on CCTV camera and, no matter how much one tries, one cannot unsee something like that. I was also witness to the never-ending zombie parade of heroin addicts as they walked past my front window on their way up from King's Cross. The writing was definitely on the wall for a change.

As the big five-oh was fast approaching, I found the noise and hustle and bustle of inner-city life tiring, and I started to yearn for something a little more tranquil and serene.

As if those reasons weren't enough, there were other incentives for moving. Members of my increasingly large family in Australia are often visiting and I want to encourage them to do so. With nieces and nephews reaching gap-year age now being added to the mix, I want to provide a home away from home for them. Staying with me also saves them the cost of finding accommodation in London, which is very expensive.

Putting up guests was always a challenge in Camden, as my terraced house only had 1.5 bedrooms – and the big one was mine! I wasn't going to part with my master suite and little cupboard en suite for anyone. The small room was the only other place to sleep, and that had been cut in half to make room for my en suite. It also housed a wardrobe that was heaving with my glitzy suits and, three days a week, the room had to double up as the office for my PA, Clare. It had a small sofa bed but when that was folded out guests couldn't even open a suitcase in the room, let alone get around it to sit at the desk.

As she got older, Mum was finding it especially difficult. On her visits, she likes to be able to open her suitcase, unpack completely and put everything away in drawers and a wardrobe. No chance of that happening in Camden. Every morning I would put the sofa bed back to its sofa position, set her suitcase on the sofa where she would take out what she needed for the day, then put the suitcase back in the cupboard and hope to God that Mum didn't need anything else later that day. Every day for six weeks! To add another layer of complexity, guests usually don't visit in singles, they come in pairs or groups, which added significantly to the logistical dilemmas. I remember that while my niece Isabelle was studying acting at the Royal Academy of Dramatic Arts, she had to move out of her room one night to make way for some more mature guests. She slept peacefully outside, on the outdoor sofa on my rooftop terrace! Luckily, it was summer in London at the time.

Back then, I wouldn't have had it any other way, though. I love being surrounded by people and offering them my hospitality. We had our challenges fitting into that little house but we are still on speaking terms and that's all that matters.

Another reason that Camden wasn't working for me then is that I am a born entertainer and love nothing more than rustling up a dirty big spag bol or curry for over twenty people at a time. The kitchen wasn't large enough for me to cater for crowds like that. I longed for the day I had a serving space to dish up special menus plate by plate, rather than a buffet style where people pick up their plates and serve themselves. Not that there is anything wrong with that but I was reaching an age where I wanted to explore more fancy culinary pursuits.

Prepping in the Camden kitchen was like working in a caravan and I became an expert in whipping up crowd pleasers in a very small space. I had knocked a wall out to fit in a dining table but let's just say it was still very cosy entertaining in my little two-up two-down.

Like myself, my pink house was also showing signs of wear and tear and needed a serious injection of funds to bring it back to its former glory. I had plans to build an extension, but there is only so much one can do before you start to overcapitalize. The heritage listing made it impossible to add another bedroom, which was what I most sorely needed, so that wasn't an option.

The other, and probably the most pressing reason, was the increasing status of my celebrity profile.

Being a celebrity today can bring with it myriad positive benefits. It gives me a platform to be heard on a number of different causes and issues. Having said this, there are some negative aspects to being recognized in the street.

In the early years of *Strictly* I could get around Camden pretty well unnoticed, but as *Strictly* built a following I was finding it increasingly difficult to do my shopping or get from A to B without being recognized. Most people who approach me are really lovely and I love people and love chatting to them, but sometimes when I am in a hurry, feeling ugly as hell, or just feeling like being another face in the crowd, it can get a bit much. It didn't help that the front door of my house opened directly onto the street – a distance of one metre, to be exact – so that whenever I opened the door I risked showing people the inside of my home, where, like most people, I like to enjoy some privacy. Paparazzi would plonk themselves outside the front of my house at all hours. One day, they chased my brother-in-law David up the street thinking he was me!

These factors all contributed to a solid number of reasons to find a new place that offered more space to entertain and house my friends and family and a little more serenity and anonymity in the process. So, in 2011, I started to look for what I hoped would be my new country retreat.

I'd been watching *Escape to the Country* for years, dreaming of becoming a country squire, and I was even asked to appear on the programme. But if my aim was to find somewhere private and anonymous it would, I felt, defeat the object to choose my perfect rural hideaway on national television.

As I was working at the Watermill Theatre in Newbury a lot, it made sense for me to look around that area. It would also mean I was closer to Southampton, my embarkation point for the four *Strictly* cruises I undertake each year.

To add to the attraction of moving to that part of the world, I was also dating Damon Scott, the monkey-puppet boy from *Britain's Got Talent*, who lived near Salisbury. Readers of *Tales from the Dance Floor* may remember that I met him on a night out in Southampton, in September 2013, and romance had blossomed.

Damon's mum, Susan, knew that I was house-hunting. While I was staying there one weekend, she suggested I look at a property she'd seen in the local newspaper, which was about a mile from their own home.

I didn't want to live quite that far from London, because I knew I would still need to travel up and down for theatre work, TV commitments and, of course, *Strictly*. I wanted to be able to get to the capital in an hour, and this place was an hour and a half away. Also, I didn't like the look of the house from the outside because, although it was tasteful, it was new, and I wanted an older property. It was on the market for £1.8 million, which was a lot more than I wanted to spend, because I was maintaining the Camden house as well. The idea was to live in the house most of the week but spend weekends in London, whenever I was doing *Strictly*. But because I was there and the house was just a mile away, I decided to take a look, and asked Damon to come along.

The estate agent gave us the address and we set off for a small village in the middle of nowhere. Yet, despite the satnav's best efforts, we just couldn't find it anywhere.

'That's a good sign,' I thought. 'It can't be found. It must be pretty secluded.'

The satnav eventually took us up an old tractor track – which is not great in a vintage Triumph Stag. The bottom of the car was being scraped by woodland, stones and holes in the track and I thought, 'This is madness. This can't be the address. It's literally leading us up the garden path.'

It turned out it was. You have to work really hard to find the driveway but when I finally found it, I fell in love. It was a mile-long, private drive that went up a slight hill, lined with the most delicious trees, which formed a dappled, sunlit tunnel. We came to the crest of the hill just as the sun opened up and blazed fully from the canopy of the surrounding trees. There was a breathtaking view of what looked like an old-fashioned manor house, standing proud in its setting of lush lawns and picturesque countryside. I stopped the car and sat there with Damon, just admiring the view. I was so excited to see more. I thought it was really charming. The fact that you couldn't see the house from the road was ideal, the grounds were beautiful, and it felt spacious but secluded.

It was a good start. But when I walked into the house, I was blown away. The amount of space was phenomenal: the living room was huge, with a massive fireplace. Having lived in London for so long, I was not used to so much room.

It wasn't long before I performed the biggest no-no in viewing houses (especially in front of an agent): I let my mind get ahead of itself and started mentally furnishing the rooms. I imagined a white baby grand piano perfectly placed in front of the picture window and my Swarovski-encrusted Buddhas sat happily on the Italian marble hearth. Not to mention my selection of white ceramic dancing pigs that had been looking for just such a generous mantle to high-step on.

Next, I entered the room that was my measure of any home of worth: the dining room. It was filled with natural light and was long enough to seat at least twenty people. Big tick there. We moved to the kitchen, which was bigger than my whole terrace in Camden. I noticed it had a fabulous cream-coloured AGA, something I had always dreamed of. It not only cooked food impeccably but warmed the whole room and I was itching to try it out. Next to the kitchen was a roomy orangery, complete with a glass roof, which captured the morning sun and had views out to the pastures. I could envision my mum sitting there all snug on her yearly visits and not moving for the whole trip.

All the rooms at the back had big double doors that opened out onto a large and extremely generous patio. I noted how well the house would work to fulfil my dreams of entertaining large crowds.

'This is a great entertaining space,' I thought. 'It's a real party house.'

Upstairs were seven bedrooms, mostly en suite, and a couple of extra bathrooms for good measure, all coming off a wide, spacious landing.

The house wasn't completely perfect. I wasn't a fan of the decor at all. I like smart white gloss enamel trims and the trims were all a natural stained wood, giving it a dated 1970s feel. Some of the doorways were too low for me, being 6 ft 2 in, which meant I would have to duck my head whenever I walked through those doors.

I knew, however, that those things could be changed and I loved putting my stamp on things, so anything like that wasn't a real issue. The place had great bones and was crying out for some CRH flair to turn it into the party house it was destined to become.

It's only a ten-year-old building, so quite new. Although I was looking for an old place with some history and character, they tend to come with problems and maintenance issues. So I imagined as this was a new build, I wouldn't have to do anything except furnish and decorate it.

Outside, there was a swimming pool which wasn't actually much use at the time, because it needed so much fixing and reconstruction, but on first impression it looked like it was in good nick. I could see an abundance of fabulous pool parties in the summer, complete with half-naked waiters and floating inflatable flamingoes.

To top it all, the house was surrounded by seven and a half acres of gardens, woodlands and fields, which is unusual for a new build.

So I loved the driveway, loved the space, the garden and the pool and I thought, 'I might have a second look at this.'

I went to view another property but it was only two-bedroomed, which was too small for me to accommodate my family when they came over from Australia. Then I decided to check out some other properties, including some of the old sixteenth-century houses which I love the look of, but they seemed pokey in comparison. Everything I loved on the outside seemed to be too small on the inside and so, as I kept thinking back to the first house, I booked that second viewing.

On my second visit, it was a beautiful summer's day. The sun was shining, the flowers were blooming and the birds were chirping, and that makes everything seem so much more attractive.

'I could live somewhere like this,' I thought to myself.

As I took another look around I was impressed, all over again, by the bright, spacious rooms. Yes, it was out of my price range, but since when have I let that get in the way of what I want? Whenever anyone questions my rather lavish spending habits and asks me if I really need that item, I always reply, 'It has nothing to do with what I need, darling, but everything to do with what I want.' They will probably use that as my epitaph. So I don't think anyone was surprised at my interest in acquiring this home at all costs. I did love it and I knew I could turn it into something really A-MAZ-ING.

I went in with all guns blazing and put in what I thought was a rather generous offer, but to my disappointment it wasn't accepted. I then put in my very best offer and left it in the universe's hands, with fingers crossed behind my back for good measure.

While I was waiting to hear, I got a taste of what it would be like to live in a big historic country home when I took a summer break in Ramsgate, with a group of my oldest friends. We rented a stunning National Trust holiday let that had been built in the nineteenth-century by architect and designer Augustus Pugin. My dear old chums and I had a riotous time reliving our youth in the Gothic splendour of a magnificent house.

As I enjoyed playing lord of the manor in these beautiful surroundings, I received a phone call telling me my latest offer on the house had been accepted and the mortgage company rang to say that my application had gone through. I felt like I'd won the lottery. Now I could be a country squire for real.

At the time, I wasn't thinking about Damon living with me. Initially the plan was that I would live there by myself. Damon was only round the corner, anyway.

But, after my offer had been accepted, Damon and I took off on a *Strictly* cruise and everything was going well between us. I began to think it would be a good opportunity for us to take the next step in our relationship and move in together. Plus, the idea of rattling around in that big old house by myself was slightly daunting. Even though our relationship was based on a mutual love and respect, there was no denying that my rent-boy past still haunted me, and I had come to realize that I value an equitable relationship where both partners contribute financially and pull their weight as far as household tasks go. It was important that any partner of mine has a reasonable level of financial independence.

'Shall we try living together?' I said, one night over dinner. 'I'm moving into the house anyway, so how do you feel about moving in with me?'

'That would be good,' he said.

'You'll need to pay some sort of rent,' I said. 'Or something towards the running of the house.'

We decided he would contribute a small amount towards the running of the house each week. That was good for both of us, because I never wanted him to feel as if he was a kept man and I never wanted to feel like I was in the position of keeping someone. I kept the amount modest as he was in the entertainment industry, too, and I knew what it was like to be at its mercy, never knowing what gig you might have from one week to the next. It was affordable for him at the time and, truth be told, I never really cared about the amount he paid. The fact that he was contributing was the thing. In my time as a rent boy I will never forget that feeling of not being your own person and having to rely on someone else. I swore that I would never put anyone I love in that position.

The moving date was set for 26 September 2014, and then the hard work began. Damon packed up his stuff at home while I packed up the London house and sorted all the stuff I had in storage, which took me about a month. On the day of exchange, the removal firm collected the limited stuff I was taking from Camden and then everything from storage. Then we had to unload and go to Damon's to load up his things, plus a big barbecue I'd bought earlier (as it was on a special offer with a £2,000 discount) and stored at Damon's parents. The whole move took from five in the morning to ten at night, because the truck wasn't big enough for all of it to be delivered in one journey.

Despite all that palaver, we still arrived with nothing in the way of furniture. The boxes were all full of little things like books and clothes and a few pots and pans, plates and cutlery that I brought from London, but I'd had to leave the Camden house fully furnished as that was to be my residence at weekends. So, when we moved in we only had a double blow-up bed that I had bought, and that's what we slept on.

That night, we celebrated with a bottle of champagne but, even after the removal men had left and the inflatable bed had been made, it was not to be a restful night.

The first thing we needed to do was figure out how everything worked and, believe me, it was complicated. There are two nerve centres to the house, one in the garage and one in an office in the main house, where the fuses and control boxes are found, and they both look like the cockpit of a 747. At this point, I had no clue how the house was run, which fuses were which, what the alarm codes were, or even how the lights worked. I was exploring the bedroom looking for switches for the lights by the sides of the bed or, rather, where the bed should be, and I pushed some red buttons thinking they might be right.

Unfortunately, they were the bedside panic alarms! Unbeknownst to me, they set off an alarm which, in turn, sends alerts to a whole host of nominated people to let them know you might be in danger. Of course, I had no clue who they were!

This wailing alarm was going off in the house and I was panic-stricken, because it was so loud and oppressive. I was frantically trying to turn it off, without having any idea how to do that. At the same time, a sister alarm activated in the five-berth garage outside and then all the nominated people, friends and family of the previous owners, were ringing the landline to see if I was okay because they had got the alarm alert. It was unbelievably chaotic.

Finally, after several frantic attempts to find the controls to turn it off, I rang the previous owner and said, 'Help! The alarms are going and I have no idea how to turn them off.'

'There's a fob on the keys,' he said. 'Just wave that at the control panel and all alarms will deactivate.'

Simple as. If only someone had told me that before.

Over the next few days and weeks, we began to settle in but I found myself really spooked by the deep darkness of the country. It was the first time I'd seen pitch black since I'd been in the UK, and probably since I left my birth town of Ballarat, Australia. And the deathly quiet was unnerving. Living in London, I was so used to ambulances, police cars, lights, cars driving past and people walking around outside talking or fighting after kick-out time at the pubs. You get so accustomed to noise that the silence feels a bit creepy, and I couldn't sleep at all. It was too quiet and too dark, and I found it quite scary. If I went outside, I had to steel myself and take a deep breath because I was out there by myself, with just open fields around me and not another house in sight. Nothing but blackness. It was a far cry from the hustle and bustle of Camden Town and it took a lot of getting used to.

Whenever there was noise, it freaked me out even more. Foxes howling in the night make an eerie sound and I'd never heard peacocks squawking before. There are peacocks on the farm over the hill, a couple of miles away, and the sound carries down. It's a really weird noise – like something out of *Jurassic Park*. At first, I had no idea what had caused it and it freaked me out.

Damon was fine with the peacocks because he grew up a mile away, but he was spooked by noises inside the house. If I was away on tour he'd call me and say, 'There's someone walking around the house.' He was used to living with his parents, so being alone in a big house freaked him out.

In the end I got used to the quiet and the darkness, and I love it now. Even if I'm on my own there I enjoy the silence. I can't think of anything better than going home, and being at home.

There were a lot of other things to get used to, as well as teething problems, which had never arisen at my small house in London.

I had to buy myself a John Deere tractor, a big sit-on mower and a lot of gardening tools, which I had never needed in London. I also had to splash out on a four-wheel drive car because the Stag wouldn't cut it on the rough country roads. It was a culture shock for such a city boy. Even though I was brought up in the country, in Ballarat,

I have lived in the city for my entire adult life, ever since I first went to Melbourne in search of the bright lights. It was quite frightening.

Because the house is so big, I had to go from single-phase to three-phase electricity which is usually used for businesses, and getting that sorted was a nightmare. There were no mains for anything except the electricity, which was only a single line, enough to run a three-bedroom house, not a seven-bedroom house with a swimming pool, jacuzzi, office, catering kitchen and garage. The previous owners had been using a generator, so when I got there I found the electricity would sometimes cut out and I'd have to go five hours without it; as well as having no lights, the freezers would defrost on a regular basis.

There was no mains gas, so to get gas central heating I had to have the garden dug up and a 4,000 litre gas tank installed. My internet is outrageous. It's either very, very slow or doesn't work at all, so I now have to pay £10,000 a year to BT for five years to rent the dedicated fibre optic line that cost me a whopping £20,000 on top to install, as the closest existing line was six kilometres from the house.

The house also has its own water supply and is not connected to the water mains. Instead, there is a well, so I literally have spring water coming directly to my tap, filtered in my own plant in the garage. If I fall on hard times, I could always bottle it and sell it: *'Put a spring in your step with CRH's A-MA-ZING Spring Water.'*

There was no mains sewage so there's a septic tank on site. There were other things I didn't know about, concerning the land. The house used to have stables that now belong to someone else but I have two horse paddocks. When I arrived, the stable ladies were coming to me with all sorts of queries, saying, 'We used to rent this from the previous owner. Is that still alright?' and 'Are you still maintaining the fences?' and so on.

There was also a right of way for walkers, which goes through the garden, and I knew nothing about it when I bought the house. Madonna had the same problem, apparently, so I'm in good company there. You can't stop the ramblers and you can't shoot them for trespassing, but their path goes straight through the property and straight through the middle of the stables, which is ridiculous. It took me four years to get the route moved so that it will now go around the property and won't be visible from the house. Mind you, in the four years I've lived there I've only seen three people use it. You have to walk a very long way to get there, so you have to be pretty dedicated.

As winter closed in, bringing strong winds, trees would fall down over the driveway and I'd have to deal with those. It was all quite frightening for a city boy, like moving to another planet. There was a lot to organize and, although I was continually working at the same time, I had to sort everything out myself because it was all in my name only, and the companies would only talk to me. I had every hassle that most people face but about ten times worse, because I am literally in the middle of the countryside and completely unaccustomed to dealing with so many issues. Everything had been fairly straightforward in my two-up two-down in London.

There was so much to do to keep the house running. I was splitting my time between the city and the country house and, at the risk of whining about what are clearly first world problems, I was finding it impossible to keep on top of everything. I realized I needed help, so I decided to employ a dedicated, locally based PA, a cleaner, a groundsperson and a pool boy (don't get the wrong impression – he's 79 years old!). You couldn't live there without them.

When the snows came in February 2018, I was snowed *out*. I had been away, filming in Coventry, and I couldn't get back home because the driveway was impassable. Goodness only knows what is going to happen if it snows when *Strictly* is on. They'll have to helicopter me out from the roof.

Despite its many teething problems, I feel a very lucky man to be living in my gorgeous country home. It's just what I was looking for, a lovely living space which is off the beaten track and a long way from the road, so it's very secluded.

I still have a ridiculous number of security devices at the house but now, when the security lights come on, triggered by some movement outside, I check the CCTV and it's usually a deer, a fox or some other woodland creature – very different to living in London. A stark contrast to a homeless bloke relieving himself on my doorstep!

The deer often wander out of the woods onto the lawn for a graze. Plus there are rabbits, badgers, pheasants, owls, hares and we also have the cutest roe deer, which look like fawns even when they're fully grown. The roe buck is readily identified by his short antlers and markings on the head, while the roe doe is smaller than the buck. In summer, their adult coats are rich, foxy red. In winter, the adult coats become a greyish fawn colour, flecked with yellow. Now I'm beginning to sound like Sir David Attenborough.

My lawn often looks like the 'new prince is born' scene from Disney's 1942 classic film, *Bambi*. It's amazing.

In June 2017, my garden attracted the attention of Chris Packham, who came down to record an episode of *Hideshare*, in which he hides in a pop-up tent to go birdwatching. He arrived on his motorbike and we went out to the woods at some ungodly hour of the morning, where he taught me to listen to the birdsong in my garden. We heard lots of birds singing in my own woods, which was a real eye-opener because I'd never really sat out there and just listened. We heard a wren singing at the top of its voice and saw a male blue tit feeding a female as they prepared to nest.

Afterwards, we scored the birdsong, *Strictly*-style. While I was unusually generous, scoring a whopping 9, Chris described it as 'scruffy' and 'scratchy' and awarded it a 1. That's harsher even than my average scoring and I told him so.

'I'd give *you* one,' I quipped. Chris didn't seem to see the joke, though, which was probably just as well.

On another occasion, a plague of frogs went kamikaze in my pool. There had been a pond which I got rid of, but I soon found out why it was there. Some friends and I were in the pool one night and the frogs lined up in their hordes, in a straight row along the poolside. Then they started jumping into the pool in turn down the line. I'd never seen anything like it. It was like a routine from Esther Williams' *Million Dollar Mermaid* (known as *The One Piece Bathing Suit* in the UK) – the 1952 Metro-Goldwyn-Mayer movie about Australian swimmer Annette Kellerman, choreographed by Busby Berkeley.

Before I moved in, gossip about the new owner of the house was rife in the local area. The butcher was telling everyone that Bruce Forsyth was moving in, so all the neighbours were convinced it was Brucie. They were probably bitterly disappointed to find out it was me!

To make up for it I decided to announce my arrival with a huge champagne reception. I went out and delivered invitations to everyone within a few miles' radius of the house and all but one of the neighbours, who was away, turned up. In my naivety, I thought they'd all turn up in country wear – Barbours and wellies – but everyone turned up in smart suits and cocktail gowns. They obviously thought my party would have all the glitz and sparkle of *Strictly Come Dancing*. Unfortunately, I was wearing a pair of shorts, a T-shirt and flip-flops. I had to go upstairs and change into a suit. Also, everyone was exactly on time which I wasn't expecting either, so that caught me unawares. I'm so used to guests in London being fashionably late.

In total, there were fifty guests and it was really lovely to meet all the neighbours in one go. It all went off very well and, of course, long beyond the ten o'clock cut-off time. My invitation said the party would be between 6.30 and 8.30 p.m., just two hours, and I had decided beforehand that I was going to kick everyone out by 10 p.m. But they stayed and stayed and we had more and more wine. It was great; I loved getting to know them all.

It's a very posh neighbourhood. All my neighbours have their own companies and successful careers and most of the houses are expensive. We're not a village because we are all dispersed around the countryside, so there are only six or seven houses within a three-mile radius.

Because of my work, I still get to experience the mad rush of London on a regular basis and, what with touring, West

End shows and all my *Strictly* commitments, I probably don't spend as much time at the house as I'd like. But when I'm there, surrounded by peace and quiet, I can fully relax and recharge the batteries for the madness of my life.

They say an Englishman's home is his castle and, when I'm in my Hampshire pad, I can truly live like a queen.

CHAPTER 2

The End of an Era

At the end of each series of *Strictly Come Dancing*, the entire cast and crew, along with their families and friends, celebrate with a wrap party before going their separate ways. In December 2013, we all said goodbye after another fantastic series and, as far as we were concerned, the judges and presenters would all meet again the following year and all would be well. We had absolutely no inkling that was to be Bruce Forsyth's last year on the show.

Bruce had been winding down for a while and no longer did the results show because it was getting too much for him. He had obviously been thinking about his future during the 2013 series because, in April 2014, two months after he turned 86, he announced he wouldn't be coming back for the next series.

Despite his age, it came as quite a surprise because, having announced it when he did, he never got to go out with a big bang and a celebration on the series and we would all have loved to have given him a big send-off. Instead, the BBC ran a separate tribute at a later date.

When I joined the *Strictly* judging panel, for the very first series in 2004, I was a TV novice and Brucie was like a father figure to me. He was so experienced about TV, show business and, most importantly, the press. If the papers were giving me a hard time, he'd say, 'Don't worry about it.' He was the one who really taught me what to say and what not to say. He was good at playing the diplomat with the press.

We all need to do our jobs and being on TV gives you a privileged platform from which to speak. Some will love what you say and some will hate it, and sometimes it is misconstrued or misunderstood, but papers need headlines.

Throughout the years, whatever problems I was having, personal or professional, I could always go to Bruce and ask his advice and he would make time to listen. If you were in a state, or something had happened at home, he would be there for you. He was a lovely guy, and genuine.

Three years after he announced his departure, Bruce passed away at the age of 89. Despite his age it was a shock. We had known that he hadn't been well for a couple of weeks but we hadn't known how serious it was. *Strictly*'s executive producer, Louise Rainbow, phoned me three minutes after I got a Google alert on my phone. The BBC had tried to tell everyone in the *Strictly* family before the word got out, but it was impossible because news is so immediate these days.

To be honest, I hadn't seen much of Bruce since he left, except for the occasional charity do and the *Strictly* Christmas special, but I felt very sad to hear he had gone. It was the end of an era and part of *Strictly* died with him. But, as Tess has said in the past, we feel Brucie's presence every time we hear the music, and his spirit lives in the studio with us. It is true, as soon as I hear the opening bars of the

Strictly theme – *da da da da da da daaarrrr* – I think of him. His famous sayings, like 'You're my favourites', come up in conversation all the time. The show is a great tribute to Bruce and will always be part of his legacy, as long as we go on.

Strictly's never going to be the same without Brucie. He's very much missed and still loved, to this day. We will always remember him for the magic he brought to the show.

After Bruce decided to step down, it was announced that Claudia Winkleman would be taking over and co-presenting the show with Tess. I thought that was a great idea because I love Claudia and I'd worked with her for years on *It Takes Two* and various other things, and I knew she was quirky enough and mad enough to make it her own.

She's a really lovely down-to-earth person who is totally unaffected by the 'business'. She talks to you and asks questions, and really listens to what you have to say and I love that about her. We have always had a good working relationship. On *It Takes Two*, I'd be candid and say exactly what I thought, and she would tease me saying, 'Ooh, you can't say that!' But of course I could, because that's what I'm there for.

Claudia and Tess make a great double act. The dynamic between Brucie and Tess was brilliant and you can't replicate that, but bringing in Claudia shifted the dynamic completely. She never professed to know anything about dance and, because of that, she becomes the voice of the layman at home. If something is a bit technical she'll say, 'Oh, I don't understand that. What does it mean? How is it done?' In that way, she asks all the questions that the audience at home want answered.

I remember her coming up to me on her first night and saying, 'Oh, Craigy' – yes, that's what she calls me – 'Craigy, I'm really nervous.'

'Why would you be nervous?' I said. 'You've worked on *It Takes Two* for years and you know all the ins and outs of *Strictly*.' But I suppose taking on the responsibility of hosting the show, going live to 12 million viewers, is very different. Like with Bruce, Tess plays the straight woman so Claudia has to be the comedy turn. Bruce's were enormous boots to fill but I think she filled them in her own spectacular and kooky way, and that's what's so glorious about Claudia.

'Just be your own wonderful self,' I told her.

It took Claudia a few weeks to settle in to her role because she and Tess had to develop a double act together and you don't just do that overnight. Ant and Dec didn't do it overnight and neither did Laurel and Hardy, Morecambe and Wise or French and Saunders. They have now honed their double act to a point where I think it could go on beyond *Strictly*, if the show were to finish, and it's nice seeing an all-female comic presenting team because it makes a refreshing change.

Tess and Claudia are great fun but they also have a lot on their plate. It's a long show, and sometimes the first time they say things is on the live broadcast. The script can be changed within seconds of us going live, and it's being typed as they speak. The physical timing of the comedy is all live, so there's no opportunity to do it again if it goes wrong.

To maintain the element of surprise, judges are not part of rehearsal so we are oblivious to what might happen on stage between Claudia and Tess. The good thing is that all Claudia's jokes are as fresh to us as they are to the viewers, the only difference being we can see the mechanics behind it. So when Claudia is doing a gag about being pulled off stage by an elephant, we just see a stagehand holding a rope and yanking her backstage. We never know what she's going to do next.

Claudia and Tess are genuinely best friends, and they're always having little parties together after the show. Claudia will corner me and say, 'Craigy, we're having a party in Tess's dressing room, you must come in.' The last time, she was really insistent that I joined her, even though I had guests of my own in my dressing room. When I finally agreed, she said, 'Oh, good, we've run out of wine. Can you bring some of yours?' The cheek!

Claudia created something unique for the show. She stayed true to herself and did both herself and the *Strictly* brand proud and, as any judge will tell you, that isn't easy.

Tragically, for Claudia, just when she was getting in her stride, her daughter suffered a horrific accident shortly before the Halloween special. As most readers will remember, eight-year-old Matilda suffered terrible burns when a spark from a candle made her costume go up in flames. We were told that Zoë Ball was stepping in to cover the Halloween special at the last minute because of a family emergency. When word got out around the *Strictly* family about what had happened to Matilda we were all so upset and in shock. Not being a parent myself I can only imagine how traumatic it would have been for Claudia.

She took some time off the show and then returned, which must have been a huge challenge under the circumstances. When she came back she and I didn't really talk about what had happened. It's so hard to know what to say in that situation. I felt she wouldn't want everyone coming up to her and saying, 'I'm so sorry to hear about your daughter,' so I said nothing. I figured that she knew how much we cared and I thought everyone bringing it up might make it harder for her to do what she had to, and still try to be funny.

Obviously it took a couple of weeks before she could do that, which we all totally understood and our hearts all went out to her. There's a lot of love at *Strictly* and a lot of open arms ready to give you a hug. It's good that she works in such a supportive environment because it can be a cut-throat industry but *Strictly* really is a loving, all-embracing family unit where everyone sticks together. That support, I hope, made it easier for Claudia to come back to work. Claudia is a wonderful, brave woman and has a remarkable resilience.

When Matilda was well on the road to recovery and Claudia was more comfortable talking about her daughter's accident, she used her high profile to do a very brave interview highlighting the issue of costumes that don't meet the British nightwear flammability standard. The interview sent an important message out, not just to manufacturers but to parents who may have put their children in those sorts of costumes without knowing the dangers.

That year, for one week only, we had Donny Osmond as our guest judge. He was all smiles and great fun but he ended up handing out the first ten of the series – in week three! The surprise mark was given to Frankie Bridge and Kevin Clifton for their paso doble, which was good but far from perfect. I scored it an 8.

After fifteen series people know my sense of humour and

know that I'm not out to be nasty but that I do like to be honest and tell the truth, as I've always said. Sometimes it's misconstrued as negative comment but we are there to judge. That all-American, 'Pay it forward' positivity is fun but if you're a judge, that doesn't work. We are meant to critique the dance and at that early stage there has to be some constructive criticism as well as praise. Donny wasn't judging, he was just saying, 'Yeah, you did great. Here's a ten.' It was hilarious.

After that, people would say, 'Is that a Craig ten or a Donny ten'? They were opposite ends of the scale. Everyone knows I rarely allow my 10 paddle an airing but a Donny 10 didn't count at all and that made us all laugh.

Viewers weren't impressed that our overenthusiastic guest had awarded the first perfect mark of the series. Twitter was flooded with complaints from disgruntled fans claiming Donny had 'ruined the show' and that the first 10 'wasn't his to give'. Poor Donny.

Backstage, Donny was really friendly, warm and lovely, just as you see him on TV. He has a permanent smile and he's so positive, very 'up' and *very* excitable. He was like a child. If you didn't know his age you'd swear he was a teenager, full of enthusiasm and love for the world.

Having Donny on the panel was fun and it added another spin to the show. I'm glad we had him as a guest because now we have a 'Donny 10', and I can use it to tease the others if I think they're being too generous with their marks.

At the end of thirteen weeks of that series, presenter Caroline Flack lifted the glitterball trophy which, I must confess, was a surprise to me, but she won the hearts and minds of the nation and that is half the battle.

Simon Webbe was amazing all the way through and so was Frankie Bridge. Caroline, who was dancing with Pasha Kovalev, was the underdog and I think that's why she came through with such flying colours.

For me, the unforgettable contestant from series twelve had to be Judy Murray. She's probably the most wooden dancer I've ever seen in my life – and that came as a big surprise.

She is so high up in the tennis world and physically fit, used to handling a racquet and hitting a ball with precision timing, as well as being able to coach people like her magnificent sons, Andy and Jamie, and turn them into tennis champions. It was quite crazy to see her come on the dance floor and make a real pig's ear of it.

Judy is used to winning, so she may not be used to people giving her major criticism. But when I said she looked 'lobotomized', she really did look lobotomized, to me. I wasn't making it up!

Judy would come to the bar afterwards and say, 'Do you have to be SO nasty to me?'

'Well, just improve, darling,' I would say, 'and then I won't be.' But it was all in very good humour. It's not my fault she couldn't dance. It's a matter of application and, in her case, probably a few more *years* of practice.

The beauty of it now is that I don't get many of the Jan Ravens – who berated me in the bar for criticizing her dance. On the whole, the celebrities don't blame me. They understand that they just need to be good in order to get good scores and positive comments from me.

Judy's *101 Dalmatians* dance was wonderful because she was playing Cruella de Vil, which is a great premise for a dance routine. It allowed her to be a bit more exaggerated and spiky, it told a nice story and the comic effect was great. It had the added complication of the dogs which never do as they're told. But using animals is always risky – as I know from appearing in *Annie*, but more of that later.

Simon Webbe was really fantastic and he had the support of his Blue bandmates, who joined us in the bar afterwards. I got on well with all of them; they are great fun and always up for a laugh, keeping the party going until the early hours. Duncan James is gorgeous and a really lovely bloke. We knew each other already because Bruno and I appeared on a show called *Scream if You Know the Answer*, where we took part in a quiz on a roller coaster, and Duncan was the host. He's another one who smiles all the time and is really easy to be around.

Frankie Bridge was fantastic and I loved her Halloween routine with Kevin Clifton to the *Wicked* song, 'Defying Gravity'. Who knew that anyone could look so amazing while painted green? She's possibly the only woman in the world who could get away with it. She's a bit of a jokester, always having a laugh and full of fun.

EastEnders star Jake Wood, who plays Max Branning, turned out to be a dark horse. The routines that Janette Manrara came up with were amazing because he's not a dancer as such, but he came across as one.

Jake's salsa was extraordinary. It set the dance floor alight and it was quite an unexpected shock. All the way through I was going, 'Ooh! Aah! Oh my God!' because I loved it. The stunts were death-defying. At one point, Janette planked and tipped backwards and Jake caught her on his foot, with her head literally millimetres from the floor. If his foot had missed her neck she could have cracked her skull wide open. It was so close to catastrophe but brilliant to watch.

The audience loved Jake and it was a great leap from his soap character, the tough-talking East End thug. In person, Jake is quite the opposite. He's a home-loving family man, a loving, caring father with a beautiful wife and beautiful children and he's very softly spoken. I expect a lot of soap actors to be like their characters, but Jake and Max are chalk and cheese.

It was wonderful to have *Mrs Brown's Boys* star Jennifer Gibney on the show because her husband, Brendan O'Carroll, who plays Mrs Brown, was there every week and they're both very funny.

Backstage there is a 'Star Bar', which is basically a hospitality marquee where all the celebs and dancers hang out, because that's where the food is. The catering on the show is second to none, and everyone gets very well fed because they need to keep their energy levels up. Dancing is hard work.

Between the Star Bar and the studio door, where the glitter curtain for interviews and selfies hangs, there's a smoking area where everyone mooches around and chats if it's not raining. People are constantly toing and froing from the Star Bar to the studio door and that's where you hear about their hopes and fears and what they think is going to happen that week. It's a really social area where you can relax and be yourself before going through the double doors to the studio, where the competition is well and truly on.

Before the show, Brendan O'Carroll would be waiting between the Star Bar and studio and, if Jennifer was there, he'd say to me, 'Be nice to her.' But as soon as her back was turned he'd say, 'Actually, be honest with her. Say whatever you like.' He was very funny and they have a great relationship, with plenty of humour between them.

Gregg Wallace took everything very seriously and he was extremely nervous. He's used to being the judge himself and it is horrible when the tables are turned, as I know from bitter experience. I was judged by him on *Celebrity Masterchef*, back in 2007, and he said some horrible things about my food and I was the one shaking with nerves throughout the whole thing. It's not easy when you are the judger judged.

For a DJ and a music lover, Scott Mills had absolutely no rhythm at all. In fact, being dressed as Sebastian the crab from *The Little Mermaid* for the Movie Week routine actually helped him. It meant he could just go from side to side looking absolutely ridiculous, and he found his niche. Then he found that there was no stopping him – he loved it. He came on the *Strictly* tour and he was lapping up the applause. Joanne Clifton, his professional partner, has a great sense of humour and she's very theatrical. She's now gone off to do musical theatre. I went to see her when she played Marilyn Monroe in *Norma Jean: The Musical*, and she was brilliant.

Alison Hammond was a huge shock because she went out too soon. She was sixth to go but I thought she was amazing and had the potential to go a lot further. She had great rhythm and she was vibrant and fun but for some reason the audience weren't voting for her.

Steve Backshall was quite wooden and couldn't dance at all, but he's a really, really nice bloke and despite his job – and his remarkable physique – he doesn't fit the He-Man image at all. He's very quietly spoken, and really kind and considerate, and you don't think of him as a Bear Grylls-type action man, who puts his life at risk by handling deadly animals on a regular basis. He has an amazing body – what we would call a 'Chock Block' in Australia, after a famous ice cream that is triangular: wide at the top and narrow at the bottom. Unfortunately, a great body doesn't necessarily equal rhythm.

Mark Wright was very cute, smiley and good-looking on the dance floor. He wasn't too bad in the end. He was our first *TOWIE* star and he worked very hard and did his best to win, but of course it was Caroline Flack's year.

In recent years, many people have commented that I smile and laugh more on camera and I think I probably do. I have lightened up a lot because, generally, the celebrities are a lot better than when we first started. If you go back to Christopher Parker in series one, he got to the final with some very poor dances, including running around like a lunatic in the paso doble. But the celebrities are really phenomenal now and they put in a lot of hard work. Many of them even try to learn a bit before they get there.

I think the Beeb have done a good job of selecting celebrities who know themselves quite well and understand what they're getting into. The contestants have learned over the years what the job involves. You're there to learn to dance – yes, you are going to be criticized, but run with it. It's the audience that decide who wins and the judges' job is really just to say what's good and what's bad so that the audience can follow it and choose the winner.

The series twelve final was a very close thing but Caroline's Charleston was really good and I think she turned a corner where she started loving herself, which is just as important as figuring out the technical side. With the Charleston, she was able to show a personality we'd never seen before.

Caroline had signed up for the live tour, which kicks off after a short Christmas break for the celebs and dancers. Unfortunately, she was forced to miss the show in Nottingham right at the start of January due to ill health, but on her return she threw herself into it and proved a big hit with the arena audiences.

When someone is unable to go on it's not a complete dance-floor disaster. I am used to having to rejig things as dancers often miss the odd show through injury or illness, but we pull it together and somehow it still happens. People who are used to working together are good at covering, so we add a few extra counts of eight in and that's what live theatre is about. The show must go on.

It wasn't the only drama that left us a dancer short on that tour. Frankie Bridge, who made it to the final, found out she was pregnant after signing up and had to pull out at the last minute. The tour producers called me to say we were a dancer down, which threw me into a slight panic, but not for long. With just a week to go until the first show, former finalist Rachel Stevens stepped in to take her place, which was a huge relief.

The wonderful thing about working in a company, whether it's on a touring production, a West End show or live TV like *Strictly,* is that everyone mucks in and disaster is averted. It's that spontaneity and sense of camaraderie that makes it so appealing to me.

CHAPTER 3

Fifty F***ing Fabulous Years

Turning 50 was a big event in my life, so I wanted to mark the occasion in style. Because I lived the first twenty years of my life in Australia and the last thirty in London and Paris, I decided I was going to have two huge parties, one on each of the continents that made me what I am today.

The first was to be on the weekend of my actual birthday – 4 January 2015 – in London.

I wanted the venue to be somewhere that meant something to me and my friends, and I chose the Café de Paris, in Piccadilly, for numerous reasons. When I left Australia in 1988, the first place I went to work was in Paris, at the Lido, so this was a little nod to my French adventures in a place that is very much a part of London, too. The first ever Vogue Ball was held there when I was acting, singing and dancing in *Miss Saigon* in the West End and I have fond memories of leaving the Theatre Royal, Drury Lane, wearing my now infamous green dress, tottering across the cobbled pavements of Covent Garden in my stilettoes, at two miles an hour, to get across to the Café de Paris. I've also performed a lot of charity events there, including a saucy show called 'West End Bares', so the venue means a lot to me.

Most importantly, of course, it's a great place for a party because it's a beautiful setting with an illustrious history of hedonism, stretching back to 1924. It was the favourite hangout of the Prince of Wales, the future King Edward VIII, and the leading lights of the Roaring Twenties.

For this reason, I thought it would be really cool to have a 1920s flapper theme. I love dressing up and the theme suited the venue's history, plus that era's costumes are easy for people to find, and the dresses are gorgeous. Of course, it was also an excuse to go back to drag for the night and become a flapper myself.

To be honest, I thought a lot of my friends would do the same but, on the night, to my complete surprise, shock and utter amazement, I was the only bloke in drag. To add insult to injury, three women turned up in the dress I was wearing – which I bought off the internet for £12. When I stood up to make a speech I said, 'I can see there are three women here in MY frock. Thank you *very* much.'

My mum Beverley and sister Sue came over from Australia for the party. Getting ready was hilarious. Mum and I were the last ones left putting the slap on in Camden because everyone else went to the venue early, to set everything up. Getting out of the taxi in the middle of the West End, I narrowly escaped getting run over by a black cab and then I was stopping traffic, dressed in a flapper dress, so Mum could cross the road. When we got to the Café de Paris I was standing on the street, knocking and knocking, and no one could hear me because they were all doing soundchecks downstairs. There I was stuck on the doorstep, in full drag, with my mum, trying to get into my own party.

When they finally let us in, and people started arriving, I was quite anxious. There were 200 people there and the meeting and greeting took at least an hour and a half. As my guests lined up to say hello, all I could think about was, 'Are there enough mini-burgers going round? Are there enough chicken skewers? Are the vegetarians being fed?'

It's quite nerve-wracking when you're the guest of honour and you've arranged the party. You feel a lot of responsibility. Plus I had my family there and it was the first time they'd intermingled with anyone from *Strictly*. Louise Rainbow, the executive producer of the show, was there, along with Bruno Tonioli, Darcey Bussell and my former colleague Arlene Phillips. Len Goodman wasn't there because he hates parties, which won't surprise anyone that watches the show.

In my line of work, you move from company to company, meeting different people along the way so, after thirty years of working in theatre, you pick up a lot of friends. Plus there are all sorts of people I've met through TV work – directors, producers, performers, etc. I also invited all my friends from thirty years ago, from both Australia and the UK, as well as new friends and *Strictly* colleagues, and a few ex-boyfriends, too. Despite the numbers, I was determined I had to catch up with everyone, so I made a point of going round to each table and spending time with each group. The atmosphere was wonderful.

I have planned many a party in my time and I thought I'd organized my 50th to within an inch of its life. But it turns out I was in for a few surprises.

Alex Murphy, who did some of the lighting and production management on the *Strictly* tour and has become a great friend of mine, was stage managing the whole thing and, as far as I knew, we had a band and a singer, Rietta Austin, who has worked as a vocalist on *Strictly* and is a good friend. I also knew that Damon was going to do his act with the monkey puppet, which he had performed on *Britain's Got Talent* years before, but I thought that was it.

Little did I know that Rietta and Alex had other plans. Alison Jiear, who I knew in Australia and has been a close friend of mine since I was 20, suddenly appeared on the balcony and sang 'I Just Wanna F***ing Dance' from *Jerry Springer: The Opera*. She starred in the show as the overweight trailer trash, larger than life, voluptuous poledancer and now sings on *Strictly*, too. She knew it was one of my favourite songs, so that was a highlight of my party. Then there were burlesque dancers and a girl who did an amazing, saucy feather dance and it was all a total surprise to me.

It turned out Rietta had arranged for the band to work for nothing except food and drink, in exchange for a chance to use the venue and party to shoot a video. Then Rietta and Alex paid everyone else from the budget for the band and what I'd set aside for lighting, and pulled in some favours to keep the cost down so it didn't escalate to £100,000, which it could easily have done.

Sue, who is an incredibly talented writer, made an amazing speech which made us all howl with laughter and brought a tear to my eye.

Craig's 50th Speech @ Café de Paris, 4 Jan 2015

Hi, I am Craig's older sister Sue. Craig's mate Magatha likes to think of me as the adopted sister, but no such luck.

As you can hear I AM AUSTRALIAN and very proud to be AUSTRALIAN, Dr Brewster. [A little in joke from the movie *Tootsie*.]

Unlike my TRAITOR brother Craig, who tarts around between both the UK and his HOME country.

Not unlike his great-great-grandfather Moses Horwood, originally from Aylesbury, who shared his time between two countries as well, although not by choice.

For those of you who don't know, our ancestor Moses ripped off a pub in Gloucester, The Queen's Hotel, Cheltenham, 150 years ago and was shipped to Van Diemen's Land, or Tasmania as we call it now. [More about that in Chapter 8.]

Sadly, the only bling Moses wore was his rather heavy set of ankle bracelets.

It is lovely for the family to be in London, all the way from Craig's HOME country, Australia, to celebrate his 50th with him. It is finally HIS YEAR!!!!! [A nod to one of my favourite movies, *Strictly Ballroom*.]

Fifty years ago, if you told me the kid who had stones thrown at him on the way to school in Ballarat would become a famous TV personality, I would have found that VERY hard to believe.

If you told me the navy brat directing a play called 'The Ghost of Sir Quackly' *at the family Christmas concert in the front room of Nana's house would become an acclaimed theatre director, I would have said 'you're dreamin''.* [This is a nod to the famous Aussie film *The Castle*.]

If you told me the state winner of Sunbeams Junior Chef of the Year, with his famous Jellied Prawn Cocktail recipe, would one day come runner-up in Celebrity MasterChef UK, *I would have said 'pull the other one'.*

Or that this self-taught musical genius, 'no lessons, thanks, Dad' [a nod to the movie *The Wedding Singer*] *who can incidentally play the trumpet, tuba, guitar, French horn, piano and recorder, not to mention being quite handy with my Knitting Nancy, would win UK's* Maestro at the Opera, *I would have said 'impossible'.*

Fifty years ago, if you told me this plump kid who rocked and sang himself to sleep every night, hugging his embroidered rocking horse pillow, and danced on BTV 6 wearing a T-shirt with two pigs rooting on the front, would make a living singing and dancing in musicals ... well ... that I just might believe.

Or that this sausage-loving sissy from Ballarat would one day be chosen as head judge for UK Sausage Week and become best mates with a member of the royal family! No way in hell.

Or that this oily teen who overdosed on pimple cream till his face peeled off, and made wall hangings out of wood, nails and string, would turn papier mâché, gothic sculptures into works of sellable art? Not a chance.

Or this hard-working kid who not only chopped wood for the stove but became an apprentice chef, hairdresser, trolley boy, delivery boy and camera boy would one day become … someone's rent boy?

Well, that still surprises me to this day.

(I told you I would have loaned you the money.)

On a Strictly P&O *cruise recently, I met a gentleman whose wife dragged him along to Craig's Q&A session. He told me his first impression of Craig was one of those pompous tossers born with a silver spoon in his mouth. After hearing what Craig had to say at the Q&A, he was weirdly delighted to hear that Craig had it tough growing up.*

That gentleman really doesn't know the half of it. Tough isn't the word.

But the first part is true.

The tosser part.

And there was no silver spoon.

Don't get me wrong, thanks to Mum keeping the home fires burning, we were all cared for and loved, but Craig endured his fair share of torment growing up. And although on the surface it might look like he had it easy, it wasn't easy at all. Over the last fifty years my brother rose above the less than perfect father, the stone throwers, the pervy TV execs and the lunatic head chefs and he did it his way.

Those who have read Craig's books know a lot of what he's been through, although perhaps not all. His is a private story of struggle and resilience that makes what Craig has achieved in his 50 years not only more remarkable but a phenomenal act of survival.

So it is fitting that his favourite song growing up was 'I Will Survive'. As he has not only survived but thrived in the last half a century, and on behalf of my family here, David, Izzi, Jenna and Thomas, my mum Bev, and siblings in Melbourne, Diane, Mel and Trent and their families, we are so glad that you did.

And now for something special.

My brother and I enjoy a wonderful brother/sister relationship, not competitive in any way. I was always the writer and he was the dancer so there was no need to compete, as this poem I have written for this occasion clearly demonstrates.

I Will Survive

At first, I was afraid, I was petrified.
Kept thinking Craig could never live without me by his side.
But he got on that stupid plane and he flew across the map
Didn't think for just one second about me stuck in Ballarat!!!
And so you're BIG!!!
Whoopiddydoo!!!!!!!!!
I had to swap my cask for Veuve to get to talk to you.
I should have left school in year ten and taken up the flute,
Then I'd be rich and famous, you'd be packing shelves at Boots.
Go on, now go!
Bedazzle your ties.
Don't turn around now,
I'm the one rolling her eyes.

Weren't you the one who left me stuck in Ballarat?
Did you think I'd crumble and let you get away
with THAT?
Oh no, not I – I will survive.
As long as I have you to stir I know I'll stay alive.
You might have crystal chandeliers and brand new
white veneers
But I will survive. I have survived. Hey, Hey.

Just brilliant.

The whole event was covered by *OK!* magazine although, frankly, that didn't make much of a dent in the bill. As is always the case in these things, you are contracted to get a certain number of celebrities to attend and they ask for specific guests. Mark Wright and Frankie Bridge, an *OK!* columnist at the time, were two of the main names they wanted – and I managed to get everyone there except those two! Mark Wright was stuck in Amsterdam and couldn't get back and Frankie, as we mentioned before, was pregnant.

As a result, *OK!* magazine only paid me a fraction of what they would have done, because you get paid on a sliding scale depending on the celebrities.

A lot of the *Strictly* dancers turned up, including all three Cliftons, Janette and Aljaž. Thom Evans was there and I had a little dance with him plus Lisa Riley, Karen Hardy and plenty more, but because Frankie and Mark were a no-show, I got less money, which would have helped me pay the bar bill, at least.

I'm never one to stint when it comes to glamour and I wanted the party to be outrageous, extravagant and *lavish* (like my drag name). Because everyone was sitting down for a three-course meal, I wanted the tables to look beautiful so I splashed out on lots of decorations, including stunning feather centrepieces which cost £400 each. The trouble was that, by the end of the night, lots of the guests were wearing them as hats and dancing with them on their heads which was hilarious, but then they were taking them home. I had to pay for all the centrepieces that went missing so, in the end, I had to start ripping them off people's heads to stop them from stealing them.

The whole night was an amazing birthday treat and felt like the perfect way to mark my half-century.

Six weeks later, after the *Strictly* live tour was over, I was in Sydney for my Australian bash. I had my heart set on hiring Fort Denison, a former prison island and military fort in Sydney Harbour that you can take over for functions. I was flying out of Sydney on the Sunday, so I needed the party to take place on Saturday but, when I tried to book the date, it was already taken for a wedding. Disaster!

But all was not lost. Because I was so determined that I wanted to hold my party there and I had more guests and was ordering more wine, the management negotiated with the bride and groom and they agreed to change their wedding to Sunday. I will be forever grateful to the happy couple.

The Sydney celebration was classier than the London bash, where everyone was dressed as flappers and dancing like maniacs. For this one, I hired a string quartet and there were manicured lawns and people milling about with their white clothing – it was an all-white dress code – gently wafting in the summer breeze. The sun was shining, it was 30-degree heat, and there was a beautiful sunset over Sydney Harbour, the Opera House and Sydney Harbour Bridge. It was stunning.

Before we got to the island, a boat picked us up and took us on a little tour around the harbour, while we were served champagne and canapés, and then it delivered everyone to the venue. There was a marquee set up but all the sides were open to the harbour to give a wonderful view from this tiny island, which is about 200 feet by 300 feet, and we had sole use of it for a day.

Rietta, who had put together a band for my London party, did the same for Sydney. My mum had a birthday cake made, which was shaped like a bottle of Veuve Clicquot, and it was brilliant.

One friend of mine, Michael Cormack, arrived late because he was performing in a play at the Sydney Theatre Company. He said he couldn't come until 10.30 p.m., so I had to hire a private boat to pick him up. He came, dressed in white, tanned and looking gorgeous, standing on the front of the boat like he was Leonardo DiCaprio in *Titanic*, waving to everyone as he arrived so he made a big grand entrance. Talk about stealing my limelight!

The original plan was for Australian singer Tina Arena to sing 'I'm in Chains' from the lighthouse on the fort and Michael, who is her best friend, was supposed to arrange that. She was going to be accompanied by naked men in chains dancing on the parapets, in homage to the prisoners who used to live on the island. We also wanted to get singer Marcia Hines – Mum used to iron her costumes at Channel 6 back in the 1970s – to sing Bias Boshell's 'I Got the Music in Me' and 'I Don't Know How to Love Him', from *Jesus Christ Superstar*, the first musical I'd ever seen as a child in Sydney in the 1970s. Sadly, neither were available to perform so that was disappointing.

Because I had been away from Australia for so long, the party was populated with people I hadn't seen for thirty years, including the fabulous Ronnie Arnold, my first contemporary American jazz dance teacher and fellow performer in numerous musicals in Australia. I have fond memories of him getting a piggyback from Dad on my 21st birthday in Ballarat before they both collapsed in a screaming heap over a wire fence in the paddock to the horror of the neighbours, as Ronnie was probably the first black person they'd ever laid eyes on. My second dance teacher, Tony Bartuccio, was there as well as his wife, *Neighbours* and *Prisoner Cell Block H* star Caroline Gillmer, plus a whole host of people who taught me or knew me from my earlier career. I invited the most obscure and insane group of people but they all got on. There was one friend there that even I didn't recognize, I hadn't seen him for so long.

People aren't always keen to rekindle old friendships but I love to. I'm a person who will go back and pick up where I left off. If I don't see someone for five or six years, I don't worry about lost time, I just carry on as before. I don't blame anyone for not keeping in touch because I have lived like a gypsy for my adult life, travelling with a suitcase from place to place. Even when I put down some roots, in Camden and now Hampshire, I was touring most of the time and I was never at home. But bringing people together from different eras of my life was amazing because

I got people coming up to me and saying things like, 'Oh my God, I haven't seen Tony Bartuccio for thirty years.' It was incredible. The atmosphere was wonderful and so was the weather.

The sunset was amazing and the breeze died down as we sat down for dinner, so it couldn't have been more perfect. People were dancing until well into the night and then the boat took us back to the shore for a nightcap.

There is a sad postscript to this story. The following day, I hosted a lunch at Bungalow 8 at Darling Harbour, which overlooks the harbour and the Sydney Opera House with Fort Denison in the background. A lot of slightly hungover partygoers met there for a burger and a drink, to chat about the party and what a wonderful day we'd had, in the blazing hot sunshine, with the cool breeze caressing our cheeks as we looked over the breathtaking scenery from this beautiful island.

When I woke that morning, my first thought was for the lady who had moved her wedding for me, and I was relieved that the weather was still fine.

'At least the bride I swapped with has a nice day for her wedding,' I said, as I greeted my friends at Bungalow 8. But I spoke too soon.

At one o'clock in the afternoon, the storm clouds rolled in. And not just any old storm clouds – literally a hurricane, bringing torrential downpours. The lashing rain lasted all afternoon and the winds meant it was almost horizontal.

I felt terrible. I'd been convinced it was going to be fine when I woke up but then I saw the black clouds descend on Sydney Harbour and I thought, 'Oh no! I ruined her wedding.'

Fort Denison was completely awash. It was a complete natural disaster. I felt so sorry for her. 'I bet she regrets swapping that date,' I thought. 'She must be hating me right now.'

CHAPTER 4

A Final Salute

f 2015 had started on a high, with my 50th birthday celebrations, it ended on a real low. On 21 December my dad, Philip Revel Horwood, passed away at the age of 74.

As readers of *All Balls and Glitter* will know, my relationship with my dad wasn't amazing. He battled with alcoholism all his life and he wasn't a nice man when he was drunk.

The relationship between us got worse as he got older. I was only going back to Australia once a year because the only time I ever got off was at the end of the *Strictly Come Dancing* live tour, when I usually keep a few weeks free to go home.

Mum and Dad had finally split after the famous 'Shotgun Phil' incident, when he went on a drunken rampage with two loaded guns in the street where I was brought up. The neighbours and my family had to hide under beds waiting for the police to come. Dad fired shots and nearly killed my brother-in-law, David. He was taken to the local lock-up, where he was held for a week. Traumatic as it was, this was a blessing in disguise as it was the start of his rehabilitation off the booze, for three years at least, but it also signalled the end of my parents' marriage.

After rehab, Dad stayed in Ballarat and bought a hobby farm on the outskirts of town, in a place called Ross Creek, located on the opposite side of town to Mum and basically in the middle of nowhere. There he built nineteen dams to breed yabbies and trout, sheep and a few other animals.

His death came as no surprise to me, to be honest. I had been expecting it for the last three years of his life and every time I went to visit him, I came away thinking I'd never see him again. I would go out to the farm and stay there for one afternoon or, on rare occasions, for one night. But he drank all day, every day. He'd get drunk and go to bed in the afternoon, and then get up and start again, so you never got to spend quality time with him, ever. There was never a time he was sober so that I could speak to him properly and, as I left Australia when I was 23, he never really knew me well as an adult.

On one occasion, because I didn't have a car, Mum drove me out there but they ended up bickering and fighting in exactly the way they used to at home. It took me back to how things were when I was a child and reminded me why I left home, because I hated the fighting so much.

My sister Mel is different. She really loved my dad, she loved that lifestyle and she was accepted completely by him. He never judged her and she likes a drink, so they had that in common, but she also likes the down to earth, outback life sitting around the campfire and that's what he liked, too.

But I never enjoyed going over there and it just got worse each year, so I only went for an afternoon. To be honest, I couldn't wait to get out of there. I did feel sorry for him and

I felt sorry that our relationship couldn't be better because he was a very proud father, very proud of everything I did. When I won *Maestro at the Opera*, the conducting show, in 2012, he must have watched it about sixty times and cried every time. He loved it. He couldn't watch *Strictly* in Australia and he never came to the UK, so he never saw my life here.

One problem was that I never had anything to say. The conversation would dry up. He would say, 'How are you, mate?' and, 'How's life in the UK?' and I'd tell him but it was in one ear and out the other. I found it easier to go with my siblings, because Mel would take over and you could spread the conversation out a bit more, but it was difficult. I had nothing in common with him anymore. I had more in common when he used to come and see my drag acts but he was a lot younger then and so was I.

As well as the drinking, he had skin cancer all over his face that had to be cut out every year so his face was looking more and more raddled and he wasn't looking very healthy.

Dad endured a harrowing home invasion a few years before his death when an ice (crystal meth) addict forcefully tried to break into his house while escaping from the police. Dad was woken in the middle of the night by the sound of heavy panting, like a wild animal, outside his bedroom window. He pulled the bedroom curtains across and in the darkness he saw a tall man in a hoodie violently throwing his body against the front security door. Dad was terrified and screamed at him to 'Fuck off'. Dad didn't like the F-word and used it very selectively, so that was unusual.

The guy was focused entirely on getting in. Dad fumbled for the phone and called the police who told him they had been in pursuit of the man and had lost him but to hold fast, they would be there soon. Dad said it seemed to take forever for them to come. In the meantime, the intruder was gaining momentum and was about to burst through the security door. Dad was convinced that his time was up so he ran to the lounge where his naval sword was on display on the wall, the same sword that Dad would only ever take out for special occasions like cutting the cake at family weddings and 21st birthday parties. This time it served a different purpose: rather than celebration, it was his only protection. Wearing only his jocks, he pulled off the safety sheath and positioned the sword between him and the front door.

Dad could hear the desperation in the guy's cries outside the door and knew that a mighty battle would ensue if he got inside. Dad was screaming expletives again, 'Fuck off, you bastard.' The intruder wouldn't have stood a chance if he broke the door down, as he would have run straight into the sword's sharp tip and that would not have ended well. Right before the door hinge was about to give way, Dad could hear a police siren wailing in the distance. He collapsed to the floor in what would have been a combination of relief and shock. His heart was racing and he was convinced he was going to have a heart attack. He could hear shouts and a kerfuffle outside and crawled to the window to see what was happening.

It took five police officers to restrain the drug-crazed intruder but restrain him they did. After the guy was thrown into the police van, a member of the police force knocked on Dad's door but Dad was frozen in fear. Eventually he managed to get to the door and open it. They were relieved to see that Dad was safe and advised that he should undergo medical checks, so he stayed overnight in hospital, just to be sure. This turned out to be a blessing as the idea of going back to that house was terrifying to him.

It turned out the police had been chasing the intruder after he ran some red lights in the town and was driving erratically. He then crashed his car, half a mile from Dad's place, and took off from the scene on foot. The police lost sight of him so had to call in police tracker dogs from a nearby town, which took some time. Dad's house was on a corner and the intruder, in a drug-induced frenzy, tried to break in to escape the police.

The next day, Dad had to go to court to identify him. The young lad with his head lowered in shame was a different person to the monster he met the night before. Dad was amazed that a drug like ice could turn a young bloke with so much to offer into a dangerous criminal. The intruder was fined, ordered into rehab and given community service. He was also ordered to write Dad a letter of apology, which we found in Dad's filing cabinet after he died.

Dad was a returned veteran – meaning he had seen active service during his long naval career – and one good thing that came out of the home invasion was he got the support he needed with the services of a psychologist to counsel him. Even so, I don't think he ever fully recovered.

The whole drama knocked Dad for six, as you can imagine. He liked his independence and enjoyed living alone. After twenty years in the navy, and many of those at sea, he had become a bit of a loner and preferred his own company. But the events of that night frightened him and shook his confidence in living alone. He became hypervigilant, he heard every sound and broke into a cold sweat with every shadow so he turned his home into Fort Knox. He built a clear glass fortress that wrapped around the entire front of the house complete with a number of impenetrable security doors. It was almost impossible for his family and friends to get in, let alone intruders, but that glassed area became one of his favourite places to sit. It captured the morning sun and he would sit on his swivel chair holding a coffee cup, waving to all his neighbours as they drove past. Of course, everyone had a little chuckle as they waved back. They knew what was really in his cup, and it wasn't coffee!

Like me, my sister Sue didn't get on with him at all. We were forced to see him because he was our dad but Sue, Di and I saw the worst of his drunken tempers growing up. Trent and Mel got on fine with him, but they were a lot younger than the three of us. I had left home when they were still very small, so I don't really know what he was like as a father to them, but I know how he was with Sue, Di and myself and he could be abusive to us and to Mum when he'd had one too many.

Looking back, there were many unforgivable moments but you just have to get on with it. We didn't exactly turn a blind eye as a family, but we put on brave faces. Like in the film *Strictly Ballroom*, we applied the 'happy face' technique.

Despite our history, whenever I was back in Ballarat I felt it was a duty to go out there and see him, and he'd always complain that I didn't stay long enough. But he wouldn't remember anyway because he was so drunk.

He became really frail in the end, like a shadow of his former self. Every time I saw him, people would ask after him and I'd say, 'I think that will probably be the last time I see him.' It's what I thought every time I closed the gate to the farm, every year for three years.

Then, of course, the inevitable happened. I was in the middle of a panto run at High Wycombe when I got the phone call from Sue to say, 'Dad's dead.' Then Mel called me, then Di, then Mum.

On Saturday 19 December 2015, which happened to be the Saturday night *Strictly* final here in the UK, my family had been around celebrating an early Christmas with him. Everyone had other plans on Christmas Day, a week later, so they all went for an early Christmas weekend. Dad drank a lot as usual that Saturday but managed to fit in an afternoon nap and party on into the night with the family. By all accounts everyone had a great time and the family enjoyed the weekend in their usual high spirits. They celebrated into the early hours of the next morning then all crashed at Dad's that night.

It was a normal Sunday morning as everyone slowly woke to get ready to go back to Melbourne. A well-meaning neighbour of Dad's dropped in to say hi and gave Dad an early Christmas present of a batch of home-made bourbon he was famous for brewing. Dad wasn't one for hard liquor, as beer was his drink of choice, so he thanked him and put it aside.

Dad was feeling a little melancholy that weekend and didn't want to be alone on Christmas Day, but he wasn't easy to be around. As happens with most families of divorced parents, it is always hard at holiday time to split between the two without someone's feelings being hurt. One parent will always miss out on celebrating on the actual day and it's always sad for the kids, even adult kids, to make the choice between which parent to visit each year. Knowing Dad was going to be alone on Christmas Day was tough and always left the family feeling conflicted. And now that each sibling has a partner there were in-laws to consider, too.

A week before the Christmas party, Dad rang my sister Sue and that was the first time he mentioned the gathering to her, but he didn't invite her along. She figured he knew she would say no and she had no desire to spend time with him as they had a challenging relationship.

She did, however, have 'a surprisingly nice conversation' with him and she shared the news that I would be featured on the BBC show *Who Do You Think You Are?*. She said that Dad was chuffed with the news but was more focused on Mum's health, as she was having trouble with a bad leg at that time. Sue responded, almost prophetically, that he should worry more about his own health than Mum's.

During the phone call he told Sue that Trent, Diane and Melanie and families were all coming up to Ballarat for an early Christmas and he was looking forward to it. Sue was surprised all our siblings were going but respected that each of us have different ways of relating to Dad.

My brother and sisters who spent that day with Dad tell me now that he was acting odd all weekend, like he knew it was the last time they would see each other. Melanie said that normally Dad would stand in the driveway and wave them off but this time he just stood there in a bit of a daze and didn't do his usual mucking about by banging the car bonnet as they drove off. They just felt like something was a bit off with him but couldn't quite put a finger on it. He spent the time just sitting back and observing and seemed a little distant.

The next day, Monday 21 December, he started acting strangely and made numerous phone calls, reaching out to old girlfriends, neighbours, his sister and his mother in Perth and even my mum, Beverley. He was fishing for a Christmas invite but didn't get any takers. He then went on a morning mission, serving the neighbours a crude form of Bloody Mary with just vodka and tomato juice – no lemon juice, tabasco, pepper or Worcester sauce. Dad apparently was drinking them, too, breaking his beer-only rule.

Later that day, one of Dad's next-door neighbours, Tom, came over to the house and for some reason we will never understand, Dad decided to crack open the bourbon he received that weekend. Being a beer-only alcoholic, this was very unusual behaviour.

The two of them went to sit in Dad's favourite place to hang out, his shed, which is the size of an aircraft hangar, and they settled in to have a snifter or two of the home-made brew. But when Dad went to the fridge to get the mixer he noticed all the Coca-Cola was gone. The home-made bourbon must have been going down well because between the two of them they drank half of the bottle, neat.

At about 7 p.m., Tom went to the toilet and checked the sprinklers. When he came back indoors he found Dad dead, lying in a pool of blood. At the time, we didn't know how he died. He was lying in front of the TV and it looked like he'd fallen over, knocked his head on the TV and died.

The last words my sister Di said to Dad on the Sunday, as she pointed to the home-made bourbon bottle, were, 'Don't drink that shit. It'll kill you.' Well, on first impressions it seemed that he did drink that shit and it most definitely killed him.

We firmly believed that we would have all the answers to how Dad died within weeks but it would remain a mystery for longer than we ever anticipated.

All this happened four days before Christmas, when I was doing two shows a day playing Captain Hook in *Peter Pan*. That meant singing Dad's favourite song, Frank Sinatra's 'My Way', twice a day. The family broke the news in the morning but I didn't tell anyone at the theatre because I didn't want them to make a fuss. I had to go and do a matinee and an evening performance and I wanted to stay strong. Somehow, I got through both shows and sang 'My Way', which was very, very emotional and it was all I could do not to break down.

At midnight, I received a Google alert with the headline 'Craig Revel Horwood mourning the death of alcoholic father'. Somehow the papers had found out and that was the story they were running the next day. I knew I had to tell the panto company before they read it, so I told them what had happened and reassured them that I wasn't going home, that I was going to soldier on. I told them 'My Way' was his favourite song and that I would devote each performance to my dad. So that's what I did and I got through it.

I couldn't leave the panto because I was the headline act, and there were no other stars in it that year. I wasn't sharing it with the likes of the Chuckle Brothers or Ann Widdecombe, as I had before, and there was no way I could leave them in the lurch. I didn't want to disappoint the company or let the audience down, and no one could have stepped in that late.

There was an understudy but *Strictly* fans had booked

to see me and I didn't want to let them down.

The family completely understood, and offered to wait until I had finished the panto before the funeral.

'No, don't,' I said. 'You need to get the funeral done as soon as possible.'

It was awful being on the other side of the world while my family were going through this but there was nothing I could do. I'd just finished a series of *Strictly* and I was on panto duty for a week before starting rehearsals for the live tour, which I direct and judge on, the very next day. I couldn't get out of that either and there was no way I could get home for the funeral.

To be honest, I had always asked myself, if he did die, would I drop everything and go back for the funeral and the answer was, 'No, I wouldn't.' When I commit to something, career-wise, people are relying on me and I knew he wouldn't have wanted me to. I thought the better thing to do was to forge on and sing his favourite tune, as a personal tribute. I don't feel guilty about that. I just didn't have that great a relationship with him. And what would I do if I was there? My stalwart siblings were organizing everything, but I could help them via Skype, so we did everything that way. I even attended the funeral by Skype.

Dad had left extremely specific instructions in his will about how the funeral should be, and it was planned down to the very last detail. He spelt out how the service was to go, exactly what flag had to be on the coffin, exactly where he would be buried, what the plaque should say and that it had the ensign from the navy on it – that was a big thing for him. It reads:

Lieutenant, SDEX PR
Royal Australian Navy

PHILIP REVEL HORWOOD
9/01/1941 – 21/12/2015

Husband to Bev
Loving father to Sue, Craig, Di, Mel and Trent
Grandpa to Damon, Izzi, Jenna, Ally,
Scarlett and Layla
'Very proud of you all'
Smooth sailing now

He wanted to be buried in his naval uniform, with specific shoes, and he even specified the socks he would wear. He wanted a full naval burial complete with the official naval flag, the ensign, laid across his coffin. I don't know why he wanted the full honours because he hated the navy: he gave them twenty years of his life but, after he left, they refused to let him come back. It was one of his pet rants when he'd had a few.

Dad had already paid for most of the funeral. He had been meticulously planning his own death for thirty years. He always used to say, 'I'll be dead by forty.' Then he got to 50, and then 60, then 70. He was strong as an ox really. Just not strong enough to stop drinking.

Even though I couldn't be there, I wanted to contribute something to the funeral so I recorded 'My Way', so they could play it during the service. It's a fitting song for the end of life – 'Now I face the final curtain' – and Dad loved it.

I went to the sound engineer from the theatre.

'I have to sing at my dad's funeral,' I said. 'But I can't be there in person. Can we record a song?', so we recorded it in my dressing room. I got so emotional that my voice cracked but I couldn't sing it again, because I was overcome. Professionally, I wouldn't have been happy with it but there was so much emotion in the voice that it seemed perfect.

'Do you want to do those bits again?' the engineer asked.

'No, not really,' I answered. 'I think that's how it would have come out on the day. I'll send that as it is.'

When it came to the day of the funeral, I got dressed up in a suit in my hotel room and the family Skyped me. I had chosen a hotel near the theatre but it wasn't a particularly good one. It was very small and all I had in the room was a fridge that I bought myself, and a bed. It was three in the morning and I was totally exhausted, not only emotionally but physically. It wasn't easy but it was worse for my family because they had to be there and organize it all.

My brother-in-law David Mason was holding up the phone with my Skype-transmitted face on it for the family so I could be part of the service and I was even in the pall-bearing procession. It really felt like I was there, going through every emotion that you would normally go through. It's quite amazing what you can do in the modern world.

Trent got up and made a speech, and my sisters all said something. Mel was a wreck throughout, inconsolable. She tried to speak but was having real difficulty getting through it. Sue, who has a wonderful way with words, gave a beautiful speech and then they played my recording of 'My Way', which was weird to listen to from afar.

Dad had two sisters, Raine and Julie, and he was the middle child. Julie gave a lovely eulogy at the funeral and told plenty of childhood stories about Dad including one about how my grandmother Phonse got her name, which we didn't know.

'He was not an openly demonstrative man with his affections, but one of the ways he used to show how he loved us was by using a nickname,' she said. 'Mum was "Phonse", I was "The Kid" or "Kiddo" and Raine had one … but we won't say, will we, Sis. Trust me, she got him back by calling him "Chook" and it stuck with him. Both Mum and Dad called him Chook most of his life. They were the terms of endearment he used, but he was also never afraid to say, "I love you, Kiddo."'

She told tales of growing up with Dad and how he loved to invent things, dreaming he would one day live in a fully automated house where meals arrived at the touch of a button and robots did everything for him.

'One of my favourite memories of him as a child was sitting on the roof of our home in Corbett Street, watching the bonfire and fireworks on the top of Black Hill,' she said. 'I was never frightened when I was with him as I knew he was watching out for me, and I felt safe with him. He was my big brother.' I thought that was really touching.

Phonse, Dad's mum, lives in Western Australia and was 98 at the time so she couldn't travel to the funeral because she's too frail. So she sat in her house with her family and Skyped in, with my niece's partner holding the phone at the funeral, like I did. One phone was me and one was Phonse and my cousins. It made us feel a part of proceedings and the only thing that I missed was a hug with my family. That physical point of contact was the one big thing missing. But it was really emotional and, yes, I did cry. I thought I was brave enough and strong enough to cope, but there were a lot of tears because no matter what Dad was, and what he was like, good or bad, he was still my dad.

The best part was seeing the coffin go into the grave because then I knew it was done, it was over and I could bury the past hurt with him. When you lose your father, it's a big deal.

Dad had chosen and paid for the plot himself and had even urinated on it before he died – *twice!* There can't be many people who have pissed on their own grave but he certainly did.

Being midsummer in Australia and 28 degrees Celsius on the day of the funeral, the gravesite was hot and dusty. Mel was distraught and kept shouting, 'The soil's too dry. It needs watering'. She was pouring water on the grave. We all reacted totally differently. Sue was surprising. She had been through such trauma with Dad over the years that one would fully understand if she felt relieved that he had passed.

At the time of the 'Shotgun Phil' incident about twenty-seven years earlier, Sue and her husband David were visiting from Sweden where they were living at the time. Sue was six months pregnant and it happened to be not only their first wedding anniversary but also Dad's birthday. She and David had to leave for Sweden a week later knowing Mum, Trent and Melanie were living in a Salvation Army hostel until it was safe for them to go home. As the eldest child of an alcoholic growing up she took responsibility for ensuring Mum and the kids were safe when Dad went into his abusive rants. She would challenge him and confront him and then once he was passed out, comfort Mum and the kids. We all had our own techniques of survival that each of us carried into adult life, some for good and some not so good. Seeing the damage first-hand that living with an alcoholic inflicts makes it hard to be forgiving but that's what Sue is brilliant at.

'Have you forgotten how we were treated as children?' I asked her.

'No,' she said. 'But it's odd because I'm remembering good things I haven't remembered before.'

Sue has since written down her thoughts on his death:

My reaction to Dad's death surprised me. When Trent and I got the call that Dad was dead, we drove to Ballarat that night. The neighbours were in the lounge room, including Tom, who witnessed the whole thing and fought hard to revive him.

Dad's body had been taken by ambulance but we didn't know to where. It turned out we must have passed the ambulance on the freeway. His body was transported to the coroner in Melbourne while we were travelling to Ballarat. By the time we got to Ballarat, the neighbours had cleaned up the blood in the shed so that we weren't faced with the trauma of dealing with it ourselves. That must have been a horrendous thing to do, I thank them to this day that we were saved from that ordeal. Earlier that night I had the unenviable task of telling Dad's 98-year-old mother, Phonse, that her son had passed away, so the thought of dealing with a scene like that was too much to bear.

The neighbours were all visibly shaken but trying to stay strong for us. Trent went out to the shed with Tom to see where Dad died but I wasn't ready to see that yet. The next morning after Melanie and Di arrived we went out to the shed and, after seeing his favourite chair, the half empty glass of bourbon on the table and the bloodstains on the TV, it hit me all of a sudden. I started sobbing. This must have surprised my siblings who I am sure would have expected me to be colder, considering my difficult relationship with Dad. But in the aftermath of his death I cried a lot, especially when we laid out his naval uniform on the bed, before giving it to the funeral director. I was just as surprised as the others at how deeply I was affected, then I realized I was grieving for the Dad that I knew was there deep down but who only showed up occasionally.

Dad had some great traits and in my personal moment of grief those good things were all that I could see. The good stuff about Dad was revealed to me so clearly, such as when he turned up in naval uniform for 'show and tell' at school, when he helped me with my school projects or when he wept as I read out my poems. They clouded the negative thoughts and erased any bad memories I had about him. All I could see was what I wanted him to be and what I knew he could have been if his demons hadn't taken hold.

My adult daughters Isabelle and Jenna were confused at my reaction and how much effort I was putting into making the funeral the best darn send-off anyone had ever seen. I think they eventually understood that grasping the good helped me better support my brothers and sisters at the time.

Grief is a strange thing. I read a quote by Bindi Irwin, of all people, that grief doesn't change you, it reveals you. At this difficult time, it revealed to us the tight bond we have as a family and that even though we all shared a father who was less than perfect, we were not defined by it.

Sometimes, as Sue says, you can harbour just the nasty thoughts rather than see the good and what that person may have achieved.

In death you tend to forget all the nasty things and start remembering the fun things, and forgiveness takes over. That makes it easier to cope. If you go through a life of blame or torment it's only going to hurt you, so I do think you have to forgive. I'm not religious in any way but I think that's one good thing about the Bible, in that it teaches people to forgive. It was good to feel forgiveness and it's important because otherwise you are going to live your life being bitter and twisted and end up a horrible person and never find happiness yourself. Then you only have yourself to blame. There is always a way out of every situation. You just have to choose a path.

There was an odd moment of relief when the coffin was actually going down into the hole. That finalized it and put a cap on it, and now it can all be compartmentalized in my head. It means I can grieve for the past, finish it, and then remember the good stuff.

As the oldest, Sue and I had been the original executors of the will but when I wrote *All Balls and Glitter*, Dad had changed it to Mel and Trent, the youngest of my siblings, because he didn't like what I wrote about him. Mel was not ready to take on the responsibility because she was closest to Dad and very emotional at the time. Trent was busy with his business and a young family and took on what he could but my sister Sue, being a born organizer, took the lead on some of the logistics around Dad's estate to support them. Sue and I were powerless to do most things because we weren't executors, so it was up to Trent to divvy everything up.

Trent is twelve years younger than me and we haven't had a lot of time together considering I left Australia when Trent was a young kid. Throughout the ordeal of Dad's death it was amazing to see him handling Dad's estate with patience and a generous spirit. At some point in the last thirty years my baby brother became a man and I am wondering when that happened.

The will stipulated that the house was going to be split between the five of us. My brother was left all the machinery and the car, and all of the big stuff. My sisters got paintings each and I got his books. Mum was in the market for a new car and Trent was very generous in giving the car he inherited to her. We were all so happy about that, including Mum, as I don't think she had ever had a nice modern car like that before. And God knows she deserved it after what he had put her through her entire life.

We went through the will together via Skype again at three o'clock in the morning, my time. I was doing two shows a day and then spending two hours Skyping with my family between 3 a.m. and 5 a.m., because that's when the family were able to get together to look through stuff, so it was exhausting, but it was cathartic to be with them, even if it was via a phone.

The girls and Trent did an amazing job: the house and the garden had to be sorted, but they took me with them, via Skype. They even took me on a journey through the house, as they had found it, and showed me the remnants of the pool of blood where he had fallen. It was like a live television feed into the house and it meant I could be with them when they were discovering things.

They would prop me up somewhere in the room while they were searching cupboards and saying, 'Oh my God, look at this!' They were finding old photos and going through bank statements, and they found loads of cash. I don't know where that went but I told them all at the will reading I didn't want anything from him. I said use the cash for a good barbecue and some beer and it paid for the estate expenses, from the wake to selling the house.

My sister Mel was a mess, and crying all the time. It really cut her up badly, she was devastated, to the point where she had a massive anchor tattooed down the whole side of her torso as a memorial to him. It probably affected her the most because he was like a best friend to her, and never judged her, or told her to stop drinking like we do.

It took three months for the post-mortem toxicology results and coroner's report to be released and up till that time we still had no idea what had killed him. He had hit his head, and he had a broken neck but we didn't know if he was dead before he hit the ground, whether hitting his head on the TV killed him or whether the fall had killed him, so we were left to speculate. We knew he had drunk most of the bottle of bourbon. For some macabre reason, my sister Sue saved the bottle with a tiny drop that was left and we tasted it the next time I was home. It was like JD Honey, which is 70 proof, but we still didn't know if it was the bourbon that had killed him. We were struggling to come to terms with the death and not knowing how he died was adding to the agony.

The first question on everyone's lips when they hear about a death is 'How did he die?', but we couldn't say. Eventually I just told people he had a bad fall and died, because essentially that was what had happened. We just didn't know the sequence of events because there wasn't a witness.

When we finally got the report, it revealed that he died before he hit the ground and that it was due to having 400 mg of alcohol per 100 ml in the body. If you consider that the drink/drive limit in the UK is 80 mg per 100 ml, you can see how seriously poisoned his body was. It killed him, just as Di had predicted the last time she saw him.

The toxicology report hit us all hard. No one wants to say that their dad died of alcohol poisoning. A drunken trip and then knocking your head on the TV and breaking your neck on the way down would have been better, to be honest. It was hard because people still ask how he died and I now have to say, 'He died of alcohol poisoning.'

I looked up a table of how alcohol affects the average person and at 50 mg to 150 mg you are tipsy, your mood changes (either you become happier or more argumentative). At 150 mg to 250 mg, you are unsteady on your feet, with slurred speech and double vision. At 300 mg, you are unresponsive, confused and probably vomiting. At 400 mg, your breathing slows and you go into a coma and die.

So you can literally drink yourself to death in one sitting. Alcohol is a poison, obviously, so it does make you think twice if you're considering going out on a binge, because that's what it was. He was used to beer and he would drink that all day, at a certain level, then put himself to bed, recover and drink again. The same, day in and day out, and the body gets used to it. He got to a point that if he stopped drinking, he could well have had a heart attack and died. His body was so used to alcohol, and processing it, that his organs needed it to survive. Even when he went into hospital for operations he was allowed to take a six-pack of tinnies in, and drink through it, because it was more dangerous to suddenly give it up.

When we found out how much alcohol was in his blood we were disappointed, shocked and horrified. But at the same time I was secretly glad that he died before he fell down, because if he hadn't, he could have lost the use of his legs and possibly ended up as a paraplegic because of the broken neck, and he would have hated that. He hated relying on anyone for anything. Plus, he wouldn't have felt any pain because he was comatose. It's better than a long lingering cancer, which so many people have to deal with. If you compare it to other deaths, it's a good one, which is some comfort. Dad died doing what he loved the most: drinking. And he died with one of his best mates by his side in his beloved shed. What a way to go.

Tom was a neighbour of Dad's and a close buddy. It was traumatic for Tom because he was the one who found him after the fall and tried to revive him. When that failed, he rang an ambulance and ran, faster than he ever thought capable, to the next property for help. He even fell through the fence and injured himself. I know he has struggled with mixed feelings about that night and what he could have done to change the outcome, but none of it was his fault. People are responsible for their own drinking habits and Dad could have had one and stopped there, but he didn't. You can't blame anyone for that but Dad.

Dad was two weeks away from turning 75 when he died and it's amazing that he got to that age, with the amount of alcohol abuse he had throughout his whole life. Ironically, when we did get the toxicology report, it said his liver was in great order. We couldn't believe it. We were convinced he would have cirrhosis of the liver, but it was fine. If he'd just stuck to beer, he would still be alive today.

Dad's death was really hard for his sisters and for Phonse, who is now 101. Losing her son through alcohol was a blow. Also, that side of the family don't drink at all. They are Seventh Day Adventists and don't have alcohol in the house so we all drink soft drinks when we visit and that's not very Australian at all. In Australia, whenever you go anywhere, you are expected to bring wine or beer. It's odd to go somewhere without it. It's a drinking culture but Phonse's family never touch a drop.

Dad adored his mum and phoned her every day, no matter what. They had a really close relationship, so it was really tough for her. But Phonse is brave. She is one strong woman. She is extraordinary.

Dad's death was like a suicide, as far as his life insurance policies were concerned, in that he killed himself through his own actions. He had been paying into numerous life insurance schemes for years, but they didn't shell out a penny. He even took one out on my life when I was 20 because he was convinced I was going to die of AIDS, because I was gay. He paid it for twenty years. I didn't die. But that was kind of weird in itself. What parent takes out life insurance so they can get money if their child dies? Unbelievable.

A few weeks after the funeral, as soon as the *Strictly* tour ended, I flew to Australia to help sort out Dad's house. There was still some stuff to clear up, like the beds to get rid of and getting the house ready for sale. I cleared out the shed and did various things to make the place saleable. Admittedly, my siblings did most of the work. I just did some heavy lifting towards the end.

While I was over there, we sold the house to a young newly engaged couple, happy that they would make a fresh start in the house that had been Dad's hideaway for so many years.

My sister Sue was brilliant, writing notes to the new owners such as: 'We've left you a bed, chairs, a washing machine, a mirror and an ironing board' and 'You are welcome to the cutlery and glasses.' Trent gave the new owners a briefing on how to use the water pumps to fill the dams, and the low-down on the windmill.

We arranged to meet the couple at Dad's house for the handover and it made my sister Melanie smile when the new male owner got out of his car and wandered into Dad's carport with a stubby (as we call a small beer bottle) in his hand. I mean, who does that? Comes to meet the old owners for the handover and turns up with a beer on the go? Well, he did and we loved it. We could hear Dad having a chuckle and we're pretty sure the new owners of his Ross Creek hideaway got his seal of approval.

It was sad to say goodbye to his neighbours like Tom and Margie and Neil. My Auntie Julie, Dad's sister, called them his village of support and they were truly the most friendly, caring bunch of people you could ever meet. They looked after each other and leaned on each other. Dad was so lucky to have had them in his life.

While I was in Ballarat I planted radishes on Dad's grave, because he liked radishes. I'm sure it's not the usual thing to plant on a grave, but it seemed more fitting than flowers.

It was interesting being there and seeing it for real, touching the earth. Going back to the cemetery put a cap on the past, solidified it, and then I could leave it behind. It marked the end of a very long journey and a struggle with his alcoholism. Now he can't harm himself or anyone around him.

As a final gesture to my dad, when the inheritance came through, I dedicated an entire room in the house to create a refrigerated wine library cellar in his honour and a memorial park bench with a plaque and a stumpery in the garden, placed directly between the sheep and the saddleback pigs, all of which are not real, but life-size ornamental garden statues. He would've loved that and seen the funny side to it, too, as he was quite eccentric in his own tastes in garden design and paraphernalia. I felt I had made a fitting tribute to him – and now I can toast him every time I open a particularly fine vintage wine, or simply crack open a beer.

Cheers, Dad! RIP.

CHAPTER 5

Life's a Drag

Between two personal milestones of 2015, turning 50 and losing my father, my work took me in another new direction that I really wasn't expecting.

Early in the year the theatre producer Michael Harrison, who I'd worked with on *Fiddler on the Roof* and *Chess*, was looking for a project for me. One day he called my agent, Gavin Barker, and said, 'I would really love Craig to do *Annie*.'

I assumed he meant me to direct and choreograph, as I had done in previous shows with him, and I wasn't completely grabbed by the idea.

'I don't really want to work with dogs and all those kids,' I told Gavin. 'I think it might be too much for me.'

To be honest, it wasn't a show that I had fully appreciated. I had seen the movie, with Carol Burnett in the part of Miss Hannigan, which I loved, so I was mulling it over but I didn't really want to direct it, so I told Michael that.

'No, no,' he said. 'It's not to direct and choreograph. It's to play the part of Miss Hannigan.'

'You're kidding?' I said.

He assured me he wasn't joking and I thought, 'Actually, that might be really interesting.' I had never really considered playing a straight female role before. I did five years in drag as the Wicked Queen in *Snow White and the Seven Dwarves*, but when Annie came up, I thought playing a real woman would be a challenge, and a far cry from anything I have done before.

Panto is different to being in a musical because I am normally just Craig Revel Horwood, speaking as me and coming in and out of character. In panto you can break the fourth wall – meaning you can come out of character and be yourself and talk to the audience – so I can let a bit of Craig Revel Horwood seep through. In a proper musical, the actor has to remain in character. You can't change a single lyric or a single word, and your timing has to be impeccable. You also have to be able to dance and to sing the numbers, as they were written.

As Miss Hannigan, you also have to have a New York accent, circa 1933, and, as she's around 50, she would have been born in the late 1800s, so she would have a really old-fashioned, New York Bronx type of accent.

It hadn't occurred to me that a man could play that role as a woman, not hamming it up as a drag queen but playing it straight. The tyrannical Miss Hannigan is the villain of the piece – just like the panto parts that I have been getting. But this was an opportunity to show that I could sing, dance and act. It crossed normal boundaries as an actor and, naturally, I accepted.

I also liked the idea of not having the responsibility of being the director, or dealing with lighting, sound and choreography. It can be stressful to direct and choreograph because you are the only one in charge of absolutely every department and it is your vision. But this was someone else's vision and when I spoke to Nikolai Foster, the director, I liked that he had a modern take on it, while keeping it very much set in 1933. Also, I would be going into the company as a fully fledged actor, which was fab-u-lous.

Once the announcement was made, it was clear that not everyone agreed with my casting. I faced a torrent of rage from female actors saying there are not many parts for middle-aged women and it isn't fair that a man, especially a man from the telly, is playing a female role. The West End Wendies were up in arms, accusing me of taking work away from a middle-aged actress who was already in musical theatre.

I totally understand where they are coming from, as I may well feel miffed if my role as Captain Hook in panto was handed to Miranda Hart. But, after initial disappointment, I would understand that this is what we, as performers, signed up to – a world that can change on a dime.

That's the magic of our industry and that's what makes it exciting. The theatre is no stranger to gender role reversal, and it is happening more and more. Productions across the world are casting females in historically male roles and vice versa. Shakespeare did it in many of his plays. Japan cast all females in *West Side Story* recently. My sister even saw a recent Melbourne production of *The Crucible* where the role of Elizabeth Proctor was played by a man and the Reverend was a woman.

To succeed as an actor these days you not only have to be agile in talent but also in attitude and accept that this is the way of the times. What goes around comes around and those with an issue could be called up for a male role one day and wouldn't be complaining then.

Many people don't realize I spent twenty years in musical theatre as a professional: that is what I was trained to do all my life and that is what I did before *Strictly* came along. So it was a matter of me going back to it rather than just being someone off the telly who had never trodden the boards before. I didn't see it as taking anyone's role. I can sing *Annie*, I can dance *Annie*, and I can act *Annie*, and I can do it differently but equally as well as a female.

In a lot of the interviews that I did on radio and TV, I was told, 'Female actors are upset that you're taking a job away from them.' I would always answer the same way. I am just filling a role and I was cast in it. If they are better than me or can sell more seats than me, then go for it.

The thing that hurt most was that some of the people making the complaints were people that I had worked with twenty years ago on shows like *Cats*, *West Side Story* and *Miss Saigon*. Yes, work is scarce, but it is scarce for male actors as well as female actors. You have to be the right person for the job and, frankly, I have a name that they can publicize to get bums on seats, as well. If that makes it a successful production, then it is providing work for the rest of the cast and crew members that might not be there otherwise. Plus I was sharing the role with Lesley Joseph, because it clashed with *Strictly* and I couldn't do Saturdays, so that opened up an opportunity for her.

The backlash made me more determined to get it right. The singing voice wasn't going to be a problem because I have a high tenor voice anyway, so I can belt out like Ethel Merman. It is not as if I was singing it as a bass baritone and, anyway, Miss Hannigan is a gin-swilling, fag-ash-Lil type of character who would have had a deep voice. A lot of women who played the role would have quite deep voices, so they sound a bit rugged and a bit edgy.

To get the accent right, I went into training with voice coach Judith Windsor for six months before I had even started rehearsals because I didn't want the negative criticism. Admittedly, I found the New York accent quite difficult. It took a lot of study, but I wanted to make sure it was spot on.

The tour was set to open in Newcastle but before that we were rehearsing in Belsize Park, just around the corner from my Camden home. I was worried about the first rehearsal because I had never had a run-through. I had done some work on the script with Judith Windsor and I had tried to get off book, which means learn the whole role, before I went into rehearsals.

When the first day of rehearsals arrived I was really nervous. Everyone was looking at me, no doubt thinking, 'He has to prove himself now.' I felt a lot of pressure. To make matters worse, the whole thing was being filmed for a behind-the-scenes documentary and that just made me doubly nervous.

After the initial introductions we all had to sit in a circle and Nikolai said, 'Right, we're going to have a read-through of the entire play and a sing-through of the entire musical, from the start.'

At this point, not even the director had heard me utter the lines, so I was really anxious. I felt that I was up against it, that people were thinking, 'He won't be able to do it. He's just another one of those celebrity castings which is going to end in disaster.'

But actually, to my relief, as soon as I started saying my lines the nerves fell away and I got into the role. It is like getting back on a bike, you never forget the feeling of being on the stage and working with other actors. I threw myself into it and we did the big read-through of the script and a sing-through as well. As scary as it was, it catapulted me into the rehearsal process, which I loved.

As well as wondering if I could pull it off, some of the actors were also worried that I might be a bit demanding, and behave like a diva. But a diva I am not. I just come in, like any old actor, and do as I'm told.

Miss Hannigan's cohorts – her brother Rooster and his moll Lily St Regis – were to be played by Jonny Fines and Djalenga Scott, and together we did our big number, 'Easy Street'. I knew Djalenga already because I had given her one of her first theatre roles, in *Beautiful and Damned*, back in 2004 – the year I started on *Strictly*. As soon as I saw her in the rehearsal room, I went, 'Oh my God, Djalenga Scott. How fantastic!'

Jonny Fines was unknown to me but a fantastic actor, fantastic dancer and amazing singer. Great comic timing. Our first vocal rehearsal, when we sang 'Easy Street', was really enjoyable, so that calmed me down.

I'm happy to say that the cast were surprised by my vocals. They were saying, 'Oh my God, you can sing!' People may have thought I was just going to speak-sing it, but I can hold a note and the three of us got some really good harmonies together. Once everyone heard me sing the relief in the room was palpable and we could get on with rehearsing what promised to be a fabulous show.

Daddy Warbucks was being played by Alex Bourne, a wonderful actor who played Darryl Van Horne in *The*

Witches of Eastwick when I directed it at the Watermill Theatre. I'd never worked with him as an actor so it was quite odd being on the other side, but we got on like a house on fire, just as we did when I was directing him. He's got a beautiful, rich tone to his voice and this mane of thick, delicious, silver fox hair which he completely shaved off for the role. It was a real shock the day that he came in completely bald, but somehow he pulled off the new look.

We had a few weeks of rehearsals in Belsize Park. It was the summer and really hot, so it was fabulous. Because I was sharing the role, with Lesley doing the two Saturday shows, we were rehearsing together. It was really odd because I got to see her performance and she got to see mine, and they were like chalk and cheese. I'm 6 ft 2 in, and in heels 6 ft 6 in, and she is 5 ft 2 in, so quite small compared to me. She's also twenty years older than me but her agility is just insane and her energy is extraordinary.

To complicate matters further, we were simultaneously rehearsing with three different sets of children, who all had to have equal rehearsal. So, I would do a scene with all three sets of children and then Lesley would do the same scene with all three sets of children. It meant the kids had more time, which is great for them because they gain confidence but it made for quite a slow rehearsal period. Then of course Amber, the dog that was playing Sandy, had to be trained and rehearsed as well.

When we finished the rehearsal period we moved up to Newcastle and started the tech. That's the point when it all became real because I was finally in costume, so I was putting the wig on, the make-up and the heels and everything was starting to come together. That's when I started getting nervous about how theatre critics would review this. In the past, they have tried to use my own catchphrases against me, rather than giving constructive criticism. They just end up saying, 'It was far from fab-u-lous,' or 'An absolute dance dis-ah-ster, darling.' Because I'm so critical on *Strictly Come Dancing*, they're overcritical, I think, of me in the theatre. Then again, I put myself out there and sometimes the critics are right and I have to agree with them.

I was expecting all of that this time, and I was really concerned and deeply nervous about what people would think of my performance as Miss Hannigan. I tried to convince myself that I'm doing it because I love it, it's a passion of mine because I know that I can play this role and tell this story. I'm just one small cog in a very large machine. It's not just me out there, there's a whole bunch of other characters, and it's Annie herself who is the lead.

Hannigan is a tough role to play in that she is only on stage for about twenty minutes, but the impact you have to create within that short time is enormous. There's not much time to build the arc of her character. Instead she bursts into the space and has to have an immediate history and set up the character while interacting with a whole bunch of children. It's a tough role in that respect but an exhilarating one.

Because of all these things, I was very nervous on our opening night in Newcastle, but when the reviews came out they were really good. They were still using my words, but in a positive way. 'You might think Craig Revel Horwood would have been a disaster, but it was simply fabulous,' and that sort of thing. There was nothing nasty at all. What a relief!

Audiences were taken by surprise because I think they were expecting me to be Craig Revel Horwood doing the Craig Revel Horwood toff accent. But I was virtually unrecognizable on stage and completely transformed, and they seemed to like it.

The show was a huge success. It had four- and five-star reviews across the board, and it was really well received and well attended. When so many shows fail, you can't ask for much more than that.

The show toured for twelve months, although I didn't complete the full run. But the adage about children and dogs is definitely true and there were a few disasters along the way.

The dog Amber, a scruffy terrier, didn't always do what she was told. Annie could be calling her but, sometimes, she would be more interested in scratching her bum or she would be facing the wrong way. Backstage, we were all told off for over-patting the dog because that makes her feel itchy, apparently, and that's why she scratches. You have to be really vigilant about who deals with the dog before she goes on but the kids, of course, loved her – a little bit too much. They were always patting her and playing with her so, when she went on stage, she looked like she had fleas.

There's a famous scene when Annie is trying to convince a policeman that the dog belongs to her. She has to call its name, Sandy – a name she made up for it thirty seconds earlier – and the dog has to run to her on the musical key change. They had treats to train the dog and make her run on cue but if Annie forgot to get the treats out or got them out too early then the dog would run and not wait for the music.

It did make the audience laugh when she turned around and faced upstage when she was supposed to face downstage, and poor Annie was trying to sing 'Tomorrow' at the top of her lungs. It was tough for the kids and all the Annies coped really well.

At the theatre, the dog has to do its business, so there's a little patch of grass on a piece of concrete that is kept outside for her. The trainer, Linda, regularly took her outside to avoid any accidents on stage, which would have been horrendous.

If anything happened to the dog, we rested easy that an understudy dog was available: a tiny chihuahua used in the stage version of *Legally Blonde*. Thankfully, Amber never needed to be replaced. Although it was touch and go for a moment there.

During the run, I had a big summer party at the house for the cast and crew and, of course, Amber. Linda brought her over early because she couldn't stay long, but then she decided to let her run around the garden and that was it, she was off chasing rabbits. Before we knew it, we'd lost the star of the show!

Linda was frantic because Amber is not her dog and also we had lost the only dog that had been trained up to play Sandy. We knew she couldn't be far away and, admittedly, watching everyone running around like headless chickens screaming for the dog had us rolling with laughter. I started to get a little anxious after a few minutes, as I realized there are no fences around my house and if she ran far enough she could have run onto the motorway.

After twenty minutes of panic, with all of us tearing about, Amber came toddling back, totally unconcerned by the drama she'd caused. Thank goodness!

The cast of Annie had three sets of kids aged between seven and fifteen, with six in each set, and they were all extremely talented. Each set had three Annies – the main one, an understudy and a third backup – because sometimes children fall ill and can't finish the show. So, more than once, I would do the opening scene with one Annie then I'd do a quick change, come back on and find a completely different Annie on stage. It was often a mystery to me where the original Annie had gone and I never had time to find out. On with the show!

There was one occasion where I went through three Annies in one performance. It was bizarre. One went off just before the show, so the understudy was on. Then I was standing in the wing with a filing cabinet and a whole bunch of kids, waiting to come on for an office scene, and suddenly the curtain came in.

I had no idea what was going on but it turned out the second Annie had a vocal problem. She'd sung 'Tomorrow', but it didn't come out particularly well, so then she had to rest her voice. The third Annie had never played her before and had only done act one as a run-through. She had rehearsed the scenes in act two, but only with understudies, not with all the actors. She was waiting in the wing, panicking, because she knew she was going to have to take over. She was excited, but fell violently ill through nerves because she had never done it.

The curtain was held back for twenty minutes until it was all sorted and the audience were fabulously patient. This gave me the chance to properly introduce myself to the poor girl, who couldn't have been more than twelve years old.

'Hi, darling,' I said, seeing how frightened she was. 'Don't worry, I'll look after you. You do what you can, I'll go with you.'

We quickly rehearsed our scenes together and she was dragged off to get into hair and make-up and a costume, and all the time, she had to try to think of what scene is coming next because she was going on halfway through the show. She had to pick up where the other Annie had left off.

When she came back, she was going through a couple of the scenes with Daddy Warbucks in act two, because they're huge. Then I went through ours again because, in the scene coming up, Annie and I are the only two on stage and we're bickering, arguing and fighting each other. There's a lot of interruptive dialogue, so she needed to keep her wits about her, plus Miss Hannigan towers over Annie which can be quite intimidating. To her, I was a massive, tall woman with huge knockers, slapping her false nails around the place and shouting, which would have been quite scary, so I tried to calm her down.

'Whatever you say, I'll react to,' I said. 'Don't worry about a thing. And if you go wrong, it's no problem. I'll pick it up and we'll get the scene back on track, so don't feel pressured to get all the words right. Just listen and react.'

She was taking deep breaths, steeling herself to go on.

'Are you ready?' I asked.

'Yes, yes,' she said, breathing in again. 'I'm ready.' Then the music started, the curtain opened, we waltzed on and from that moment on, the show did not stop. But she was absolutely brilliant. There were a few odd moments that I had to pick up the dialogue and I was expecting I'd have to ad-lib a little because even the adult actors mess up sometimes – I am guilty as charged. But this young girl was remarkable and I really hope her parents got there that night in time to see a star in the making.

During one show, I skipped a whole chunk of the scene. I made my entrance and, as I flung open the door, I said the lines from halfway through the scene, leaving out a really important part of the story. Then I had to go back and try to fill in the gaps, which is really confusing and pretty horrifying. Annie is so beautifully written and so well constructed that you have to stick to the script, not just because the lines matter but because the lighting cues and sound cues are based on the words that you're saying. If you say something different, then everyone, the whole technical crew, won't know what's going on.

All the kids were wonderful, and really respectful. Before working with them we all had to have a CRB (Criminal Records Bureau) security check – or DBS (Disclosure and Barring Service), as they are now known. Also, there are a lot of restrictions on how you connect with the children. For example, they can't give you a card and you can't give them a card or present. Anything like that would have to go through their chaperone. If they want me to sign anything then the chaperone needs to come to me with it. You can talk to them but, in normal theatre, there's a lot of swearing and a lot of mucking about and, obviously, when you've got that many kids in the company, you can't do any of that. You always have to mind your Ps and Qs, which is a good thing.

The young cast were really professional and they didn't muck about at all. The chaperones were quite strict with them but they were enjoying it and they knew the drill. They were amazing dancers, amazing singers and really good little actors.

The little Mollys were always funny because they were all tiny. Molly is the little cute one with the high voice who takes off Miss Hannigan and becomes the drunken, tyrannical Hannigan with a mop on her head, and then she gets put in the laundry basket, so she is always played by the smallest child. They were all little characters and with totally different personalities.

There was one that was always talking, talking, talking, talking, talking. I like to use any spare time in the wings to practise lines and think about what's ahead, but if this little Molly was sitting next to me forget that idea. In one scene we were wheeled on stage sitting on a desk while I picked nits out of her hair. After picking out her nits, I have to hit Molly over the head with a newspaper and tell her to 'scram'. In one show, I said 'Get out of here' instead of 'scram', and she kept sitting there and I kept hitting her and saying, 'Get out! Get out!' wondering why she wasn't moving. Turns out she had been so drilled to hear the word 'scram' that she wouldn't move until she heard it!

I did feel sorry her. She got belted over the head with a rolled-up newspaper about three times before I came out with the word 'scram' and she finally left the stage.

She was a real chatterbox and never stopped asking questions. I could have a full-on adult conversation with this child, which was hysterical.

She would tell me, 'I've got a movie coming up after this and I'm doing this and I'm doing that and I've got a little bit more training. Of course, I've got all my schoolwork which is going really well …' A lot of the kids were really quiet and don't speak at all until you come on stage. But, bless her, this little Molly never stopped.

I spent the whole summer of 2015 as Hannigan, travelling to Manchester, Liverpool, Newcastle and all over the UK,

ABOVE: Keep dancing! The judges, presenters and contestants join in the signature dance at the end of a show.

BELOW: The judges: Me, Darcey Bussell, Shirley Ballas and Bruno Tonioli.

The legend that is Bruce Forsyth with lovely Tess Daly.

ABOVE: Judy Murray as Cruella de Vil with Anton du Beke.

RIGHT: Will Young and Karen Clifton's fiery tango.

ABOVE: The class of 2016, Series 14, (left to right): Melvin Odoom, Anastacia, Greg Rutherford, Laura Whitmore, Daisy Lowe, Ed Balls, Louise Redknapp, Danny Mac, Tameka Empson, Will Young, Ore Oduba, Claudia Fragapane, Judge Rinder, Lesley Joseph and Naga Munchetty.

BELOW: The amazing 2016 finalists: Danny, Louise and Ore.

Strictly Halloween Week.

LEFT: Frankie Bridge as the Wicked Witch of the West from *Wicked!*

BELOW: Scott Mills as Uncle Fester from *The Addams Family.*

LEFT: Fang-tastic dahling! Bruno and I make very convincing vampires.

THIS DIVA'S GOT A SECRET... AND IT'S NUN OF YOUR BUSINESS

Jamie Wilson presents the Curve production

Sister Act

A DIVINE MUSICAL COMEDY

Starring **Alexandra Burke**

Directed by **Craig Revel Horwood**

RIGHT: Alexandra Burke was fabulous in this stage musical of *Sister Act*, which I directed and choreographed.

BELOW: Me as the formidable Miss Hannigan in the stage production of *Annie*.

LEFT: Me in drag again! This time as Wonder Woman for the *Annie* tour superheroes party. With me is John Mannion, head of wigs and wardrobe.

RIGHT: Me as the Queen of Hearts on another normal night of the *Annie* tour.

Which one is the real Craig? My fabulous Madame Tussauds waxwork at the Blackpool Tower Ballroom.

performing at wonderful, big venues for a week at a time. It was great to be touring again and to be on the road with a family of actors. I'd missed that because in the West End, it's different. You come in for the show and go home straight afterwards, so you don't socialize so much.

On tour, you're travelling together like gypsies, a touring ensemble, and you get to know the company really well. You end up eating with them and arranging different places for various meals. We were all in an *Annie* WhatsApp group, so if someone found a fantastic restaurant, we'd use the group to meet up during the day for lunch before the show.

I don't have a family in the UK at all. I have a small nucleus of friends and I have my theatre family, so that fills a void and, because of the time you spend together, you become very close.

Another thing I enjoyed was seeing all the various theatres, many of which I had worked in but always as a director or choreographer. I had never been in dressing room number one and been the star of the show and played to packed houses. It was a whole new experience and I fell in love with theatre all over again because of it.

My run in *Annie* continued while I was doing *Strictly*, until mid-November, when I had to start rehearsals for panto. Then Lesley Joseph took over the whole show for a while.

It was difficult leaving and handing it over to someone else, but that's the way it is, and my contract was up. So, with a heavy heart, I hung up my bra and boobies, and my heels and lashes were packed away in a box, never to be seen again.

Or so I thought.

*

The *Strictly* class of 2015 were a mixed bunch. Some of them were brilliant fun and I clicked with them immediately but with others, it took a bit longer to get to know them.

Iwan Thomas wasn't the best on the dance floor. He had the self-belief that a sportsman needs to get to the top but it didn't always translate to the dance. He definitely had the right mental attitude but not the talent so, sadly, he was first to go.

Another sportsman who didn't fare well that year was the boxer Antony Agogo. He had injured his shoulder and had an operation three weeks before he started. He couldn't box for sixteen weeks so he decided to do *Strictly*. Perhaps he thought, 'It's only dancing. It won't be that demanding.' He must have thought he could get away with a few step ball changes around the dance floor and there wouldn't be any stress at all, but of course he couldn't perform a lift or use that arm in any choreography.

It was a shame for Oti Mabuse because it was her first year and she is so talented, but she couldn't really shine.

Peter Andre is a really lovely guy and we got on fantastically well. He tried really hard and took it to heart because he wanted to do so well and get on as far as possible in the competition, but it wasn't to be.

At the other end of the scale was Ainsley Harriot. He was perfect for *Strictly Come Dancing*, because he didn't take it seriously at all. He was a joy to be around backstage because he is always laughing, always joking and if the dance went wrong he would laugh it off and say, 'Yeah, that was bad but I will do better next time.' That is a perfect attitude. Natalie Lowe, who is a brilliant teacher, was fantastic with him and she had a great time.

Another one I adored was Carol Kirkwood. I was disappointed she only got to week seven but not because of her dancing, which wasn't perfect, but because I loved her.

After the show, in the bar, she would come and sit on my knee and say, 'I know you said terrible things about me, but Craig, I love you. You're so handsome, you're gorgeous, I love you, Craig.' She was hilarious, all the time. I could completely slate her and, at the bar, she would still be happy, having a drink, having a laugh. That's the way I think it should be. It is an entertainment show. Why get so serious?

I do understand there are 12 million people watching, the pressure is mounting and everyone wants to get to that final. But whatever it means to them, even if they are just doing it for the money, my advice is to be light about it, enjoy it. Accept the challenge, accept the criticism and get on with it.

Jeremy Vine made me laugh because he was always picking me up on my grammar. I loved him, though, because he is super intelligent, very well read and I could listen to his voice and his opinions forever, which is why I love his radio show.

Jeremy knew exactly what the show was, and he knew how to play the game. Yes, he was tall, he was lanky, he was a bit ridiculous-looking for a ballroom and Latin dancer – like a stork struck by lightning, as I said at the time – but he went for it, 100 per cent.

Anita Rani is very determined, and she knows exactly who to go to in order to get what she wants. Away from the show she is very inquisitive and asks a lot of questions and initially I found that a bit strange. But then she does come from a journalist background. I didn't feel that I really got to know the real Anita until she came on the live tour. On the tour she let her guard down and became more herself and it was lovely to see her true nature inside. I didn't know how to take her until then. She was always smiley, though.

That year Anton du Beke had his best shot at the trophy for years, with Katie Derham. It was great to see him dancing with someone younger and more agile than his usual partners, the Ann Widdecombes of this world. While I love the comedy Anton adds to his dances, it was refreshing to see his more elegant dances with Katie, and to see him in the final for the first time. They scraped through in the dance-off and they didn't really stand a chance against Georgia May Foote, Jay McGuinness and Kellie Bright. I loved Katie. She was down to earth. I really, really wanted to give Katie 10s, but there was no possible way that was ever going to happen and obviously they were first out in the final.

Georgia and Giovanni were gorgeous in the final but were outclassed by both Kellie and Jay. Kellie was like a fire rocket and Kevin Clifton's routines were wonderful for her. Their Charleston-inspired show dance on the railway tracks to 'Ding Dong Daddy of the D Car Line' was absolutely phenomenal. But Jay McGuinness's jive in Movie Week blew the nation away and they loved him in the final so he and Aliona Vilani walked away with the trophy.

Jay was an introvert and came across as really quiet and shy so it was hard to get to know him well. Even on the tour, he kept himself separate from the rest of us but maybe that was his way of coping. In The Wanted he always appeared to let his bandmates hog the limelight and he seemed to be uncomfortable about being the one in a spotlight now. But his amazing jive brought the house down every night.

Aliona, who had won before with Harry Judd, became

the only professional to take home two trophies from the show and she quickly announced she would be leaving. Talk about quitting while you're ahead.

Ola Jordan, on the other hand, threw in the towel after she and Iwan were voted out first. She had stuck it out for two years after her husband James left the show but finally quit after giving an interview accusing the judges of fixing the score to keep contestants in. Dull.

I can assure everyone who watches the show we have never fixed anything in our lives. Our scores are honest reflections of what we see in front of us, and the producers give us no direction whatsoever as to what score we should award the dances.

I do have empathy for James and Ola because they played their cards in the wrong way. You can leave *Strictly* and still be nice about it. The show gave them a platform and made them famous, which they should be happy about because I think they have a lot to offer. They are very talented, as a duo.

After *Strictly*, they chose to go down the reality show route, doing *I'm a Celebrity Get Me Out of Here* and *Big Brother*, in order to keep the public attention. Without the *Strictly* wage, and the security, then you do have to become something else. I think James found that hard when he first left, although Ola is now a judge on *Dancing with the Stars* in Poland, so she is keeping her hand in.

The spats between myself and James have been well documented. There's no real sense of hatred or animosity and, in my opinion, his comments about me are a way of gaining publicity and press. In person, we actually get on. That is the truth. But he has a temper and a tendency to go off on one.

I have seen that first-hand but all the jibes about me are largely unfounded. The beauty is that I really don't care because it doesn't actually affect me. It seems some in the television industry believe the hype and think a big fight is going to break out if we ever see each other.

During a recent filming of *Celebrity Juice*, we were appearing in different shows that were being shot on the same day. I wasn't told they were there but suddenly a bodyguard appeared outside my dressing-room door. When I asked why, they told me it was because James and Ola Jordan had arrived and were five doors down from me, which made me absolutely howl with laughter. I thought, 'Things aren't that bad between us.' But it's funny that it had escalated into that.

The fact is that James is extremely opinionated and so am I. We were probably never going to be the best of friends but I bear him no ill will and wish them both the best.

CHAPTER 6

Scott Free

D amon and I settled into the Hampshire house to enjoy our new life in the country and, initially, all was going well. But after a few months cracks began to appear in the relationship. I was ridiculously busy at work and he was getting work less frequently, so I think there was some rivalry there. He had been making a steady career out of his puppet act, Bubbles the monkey, the act made famous by *Britain's Got Talent*, but bookings were starting to slow down. He had other puppets in his act but I think it was ready for a revamp or a reinvention and he needed to bring something different to draw the crowds.

It is a challenge when both partners in a relationship are in the same business, especially show business. It can be a good thing in that they both have an understanding of the ups and downs but I think there is an element of competition that comes with that. Damon enjoyed some great benefits from his fifteen minutes of fame coming out of *BGT* but it is important to keep that momentum going and he never did. With bookings slowing down for him and things ramping up for me with theatre work and TV appearances, I think that put pressure on us as a couple.

It's difficult to put my finger on what exactly went wrong and why our relationship faltered. Things broke down slowly, to the point that we were living in separate parts of the house. That's how bad it was. It was a big house so you could go for hours not seeing each other. There were no huge rows, no massive dramas. We just gradually drifted apart. On the outside it was always lovey-dovey and wonderful but as soon as we walked back into the house, we became separate. He would retreat into the lounge and watch TV and I would go to bed. It was no way to live and we weren't good for one another.

By the end of 2015, things were really strained. I was stuck in the small hotel in High Wycombe over Christmas, while I starred in *Peter Pan*. It can get quite lonely and claustrophobic in those small hotel rooms day in day out, and he hadn't come to visit me at all over that time. But the real game changer was the day I found out my father had died and he didn't volunteer to come or offer up any sort of support or comfort. I began to think, 'What's this about? This is no relationship at all.'

Six weeks later, in February 2016, I was winding up the *Strictly* tour at Wembley with the usual wrap party and, although things were tense between us, I was thrilled when Damon decided to come along with his family. Unfortunately, the night ended in a huge blowout between us, with him accusing me of controlling him, and that proved to be the final straw.

'You're stopping me getting work,' he said.

'How is that possible?' I replied.

I was furious. I had been worried about him brooding around at home and not getting a lot of work so I had tried to help him and had been talking to a friend of mine who owns a voice-over agency, to see if he could give Damon some work. When he performed at my 50th, I even paid him an appearance fee. But he accused me of wanting to keep him at home to run the house like some sort of downtrodden housewife, which was totally untrue.

The row escalated and I stormed out and left him and his family at the party, which I felt terrible about, but I'd had enough. That was the last time I saw him.

I stayed the night at the hotel and the next day, a Friday, he wouldn't answer any of my calls and I didn't speak to him on Saturday, when we were doing the final show at the O2.

When I arrived home on the Monday, steeling myself for a difficult conversation, he was gone. He had packed up everything and moved out before I had a chance to talk to him.

The only thing he left behind were two massive photographs of the dogs, 8 feet tall by 6 feet wide, that were screwed to the wall in the orangery. I eventually had them taken down and sent to his house.

The really sad thing was he took both our pet Cavaliers – his dog Sophie, who has since passed away, and our little Charlie, who we called Charlie Revel. To add insult to injury, he later renamed Charlie after his new boyfriend. I do miss the pitter-patter of tiny paws in the house but as I am away from home so often I could not have cared for them properly, so not having to worry about a dog is a blessing in disguise.

Although I hadn't expected him to be gone, the relief I felt was extraordinary. I must have got to the point where it felt normal living with tension and I never really questioned it. All I could think was 'Thank God!' It was like a big weight had been lifted from my shoulders.

I wasn't prepared for what happened next, though. Three months after the split, I was away on a P&O cruise and sightseeing in Barcelona when I walked past a news stand to see that Damon and I were splashed across one of the newspapers.

It turned out Damon had taken the coward's way out and made himself a bit of money by selling our story to the press. He told them vile untruths about me and for what? A bit of extra cash.

The worst thing was that my family got word of it in Australia and it really hurt them, because they had spent some great times with Damon in the past and had grown attached to him. My mum once joked to Damon, 'If you and Craig ever split up, we are taking you in.' At least I hope she was joking!

My sister Sue was furious and hurt at the same time. Not only because she felt like he betrayed the family by dishing the dirt on his life with me all over the tabloids but also because he was accusing me of being an alcoholic and the coroner's report on my dad had only just come through that week, concluding he had died of alcohol poisoning. Sue was so rattled she wrote to him and told him how disappointed she was. She wasn't the only sibling to get involved, but more on that later.

Luckily for me, I don't think many people believed it because he just sounded like a bitter ex trying to get back at someone for his own failed career. That's Damon's biggest problem – himself.

For my part, the article just made me sad. It's a really sorry state of affairs when someone needs money so much or has so much hate in them that they have to resort to those depths. But it didn't affect me in any way, shape or form so, after careful consideration, I decided it wasn't worth suing or even giving my side of the story. In fact, I think it just highlighted how susceptible celebrities are to people making up lies about them and having them printed in the paper. As soon as he took money for that article, he lost the moral high ground. If he had really been in love with me, and I truly was the nasty alcoholic he painted me as, why wasn't he trying to help me instead of going against me and going to the papers? It could only be to make a fast buck, in my opinion, and it was really disappointing, but I chose not to care about it.

The day after the article his brother, Justin, wrote me a beautiful, supportive email, which made me feel so much better.

He said: 'I do hope that this quickly passes by, so you can move on with your life and very successful career. Take care and all the best.'

I was so touched by the message and I replied: 'That's the best email I've had and cheered me up no end. Love to you and your lovely family CRH xxx'.

It's always a shame when things don't work out with couples and it also has a ripple effect on those around them, especially families. Before the split, I got on well with Damon's parents. We had been to Paris with them and they came on one of the cruises, where they met my mum.

But when Mum came over in 2017, being the lovely lady that she is, she thought it might be nice to let bygones be bygones and drop in to say hi to Damon's mum and dad at the hotel they ran. She figured the sins of the son shouldn't be visited upon the parents, so why not? But for some reason or another they wouldn't see us. It was a shame because I liked them and I don't blame them for any of it. They're his parents and, naturally, they will have his back.

I have sometimes wondered if our whole relationship was based on a lie because Damon swore he had no idea that I was on TV when we met but seeing how much TV he watched during the course of our relationship, I find that very hard to believe.

None of that matters now. We had our time together and it's over. We weren't helping each other so I'm glad that finished and he got on with his life. He got a new boyfriend a month later and he's still with him, so I hope that his life is better than it was when he was with me.

At the end of the day, I wish him nothing but good luck and I hope he finds something to make him happy.

I like sex as much as the next person and I believe it is an important part of any relationship but being in a loveless relationship, like I was for two years, can take its toll on your sexual confidence. I am a stickler for fidelity and would never cheat on anyone, no matter how bad it got. I know only too well what it's like being on the other side of infidelity and it's torture. I want romance in a relationship and it's always a bonus if a partner I am with instigates sex, otherwise I end up feeling I am hideously unattractive.

For me, it's really important in a relationship to have a decent sex life and if that's not happening you should talk about it, but we never did. What led me to accept a loveless relationship over those two years is beyond me but I think I was hoping things would improve. Love is blind in that respect.

In the wake of my break up with Damon I found myself suddenly 'Scott free' and my life changed dramatically.

My first sexual encounter, post Damon, was the best encounter I've ever had, probably because I'd been virtually celibate for two years. It happened with an FWB (Friend with Benefits). We spent the night together, we had the most amazing time and it was the first time I had felt wanted, and touched, for a long time. I realized I had completely forgotten how wonderful a sexual relationship is, and someone who fills the house with love and spirit.

The surprises continued the next morning as I followed the notes of a piano melody coming from my new grand piano (the white baby grand I had instantly imagined when I first saw the house). I bought it because I love music in the house, but the only thing I can play is 'Chopsticks' and my sister Sue's favourite, 'The Apple Tree Swing'. I felt like I was floating down the stairs like Scarlett O'Hara in *Gone with the Wind* towards my very own yummy Rhett. The house that had been so cold and devoid of warmth was suddenly full of love, life, vitality, music, theatre, singing. It was amazing. It changed my life.

'This is what a relationship should be about,' I thought. 'Not avoiding each other around the house.' Yes, I have a big house, and you can avoid each other if you want to, but that's no way to live. I have a lovely home and I realized it can be full of love, laughter and music instead of depression and dark clouds.

At that point, I decided that's what life should be like and that I needed someone like that in my life – not the FWB because that's not his role. With an FWB you are really good mates and sometimes you have sex, but there's no attachment, no buying each other flowers, no ring sharing and you don't have to say 'I love you'. You just meet each other once in a blue moon and have a good time. A lot of my friends have one.

Even so, the experience was incredibly freeing. I felt light-headed, giddy, like a teenager again. I was in heaven. I didn't want that feeling to stop so I continued searching for it. This desire to explore a more liberated sexual side led to me meeting up with more and more people happy to help me do just that, over the next few months. As a single person, I was now free to have sex with whoever I wanted. I was just going out and enjoying myself for the first time in ages. I was loving being single.

I was sexually reawakened and felt attractive again, I felt wanted again, I felt young again. I had a new spirit in me and I had a spring in my step. I didn't realize my self-esteem had been so affected either. In the early days of being single again that self-fulfilling prophecy takes hold whereby I believed I had no sexual chemistry and was unattractive and I am sure that's why others stayed away. I have to thank my lovely FWB for getting me out of that terrible time and introducing me to another world, a world that I had forgotten about.

It set me on a path to some wonderful experiences that became almost an addiction for me. Before I knew it, I was making eyes at people at parties and hooking up with randoms. I was loving myself silly.

I'm not by nature a promiscuous person and I would never cheat on anyone, but I was enjoying the experience of being free, being single and not having to account for my actions. As long as it's between consenting adults and nobody is being hurt, then why not?

I went on the dating website Match.com and I had a few hook-ups on that, which was lovely.

On some dates I could tell they weren't interested in me but rather they were interested in *Strictly* and would ask what Brendan is really like, or is Aljaž as handsome in the flesh. That sort of thing.

I met a Frenchman, a teacher, who was absolutely gorgeous and we dated for about three months. He had no idea I was on the telly and I quite liked that. He was absolutely adorable and I liked him a lot. He used to be a dancer and we had a lot in common, but I didn't feel ready to have a boyfriend or settle down again. I was enjoying my freedom too much. I was regaining my sense of self-worth and learning to love myself again. I was loving the exploration and feeling so attractive, picking up 25-year-olds and 30-year-olds, I didn't want to stop.

The Frenchman and I are still in touch as friends, which is wonderful.

After a few adventures, my sexual exploits had peaked and I must admit I was having the time of my life. But the novelty soon wore off and I began to long for the intimacy and cosiness that a proper relationship brings.

I needed to finally escape from a relationship which was not working and was all about pretence. It took a while for me to get it out of my system but, once I'd had my fun, I was ready to look for Mr Right again.

At the same time as finding my feet in the dating world, I was also falling in love with my house all over again because it was the first time I'd lived in it alone. It was like a huge weight off my shoulders. I think a lot of people are scared of living alone but I absolutely love it. I have good friends around me who are a constant stream of fun and humour and excitement and am happy being alone, and getting a good book out, or sitting by the pool or in the garden and feeling peaceful.

I'm not a loner. I love having people around me but I also cherish the odd day that I get to spend time alone at home. Crazily enough, in four years, I've had just four days when I've actually been alone at the house. As many reading this book will know, it's wonderful to get that moment by yourself and just exhale. It means you can do anything you like. You can just have a quiet moment, which is like gold dust for me.

The house had been fantastic to live in despite the early teething problems and I was loving that it had only been built ten years before as it wouldn't be besieged by the issues old houses face. Little did I know.

In the early spring, when I was doing some washing in the laundry room, I noticed a chalky powder on the tiles. I put a black top down, after pulling it out of the dryer, and when I picked it up I had to dust it off.

'What is that?' I thought. 'I've just cleaned here.' So I cleaned the area again, thinking it was washing powder, but it kept happening. Then I noticed that in between the tiles, there was white powder forming on the grouting. A few days later it started spreading over the tiles, so I thought, 'That's weird,' but I still didn't know what it was.

Suddenly, I heard a hissing sound, like a leak, coming from inside the walls so instantly called a plumber round and he said there was a leak in the pipework. He fixed a two-foot section and I assumed that was the end of it.

Days later, another leak appeared when I flushed the toilet in one of the bathrooms, but this time it started flooding the floor, so I got an emergency plumber out to fix that.

But no sooner was one section of pipe being replaced, than another hole would appear in another pipe. It was frustrating, but every time I got it fixed, I hoped that was the last of it. It must have been riddled with holes.

After a couple of weeks with no apparent problems, I went down to the laundry again and this chalky stuff was everywhere, and had completely covered the floor. I couldn't work out what it was or where it was coming from. I cleaned it every day but it kept reappearing. Then I noticed that little white crystals were building up on the grouting of the floor tiles and they were growing upwards, like stalagmites. I knew that the house was built on chalky ground and wondered if chalk was coming from underneath the floor. But with the stalagmites I'd scrape them off and clean and they'd come back.

One morning, I came down and the stalagmites were an inch high, and spreading further afield. I had no idea why. I moved to another part of the floor, stood on a tile, and then I saw water in between the cracks. I moved my foot again and the tile made a definite squelching sound.

Back came the plumber who said, 'Oh, mate, I'm going to have to pull up the floor in the utility room. Is that alright?'

But that was just the beginning.

'I've got some bad news,' he said. 'It's flooded, completely waterlogged throughout the whole of this room.'

'Where's it from?' I asked.

'It must be a pipe somewhere,' he said. 'But I need to pull the rest of the floor up to investigate.'

It turned out that the whole of that part of the house was completely flooded underfloor and had been leaking slowly, probably for years. The piping was cheap copper from China, or so the builders said, and it had leaked. The 'stalagmites' were salt and water reacting with concrete and corroding the copper pipes further.

In the end, the whole of the flooring had to come up, the foundations were dug down, all the skirting boards had to be replaced. It took four months to dry out and then eight months to rebuild.

In the meantime, I couldn't live there because there was no kitchen, no hot or cold water, no heating and no water pipes. I had to have a brand-new kitchen, utility room and bathroom done. The insurance company paid for the essential work but I used the opportunity to upgrade at my own expense, to get it the way I wanted.

By this time, Janette and Aljaž were renting a room in my London house, so I was homeless. The London house only had two bedrooms and Janette and Aljaž often had other guests so I couldn't stay there. I had all my stuff – including all my *Strictly* costumes – and there was no way I could fit it all in the Camden house, while they were renting, too.

Faced with a year with nowhere to live, I based myself in the penthouse suite at the Holiday Inn in London, which gave me a completely different view of Camden than I had had for the last twenty-six years. Then I took every *Strictly* cruise I could, just to have somewhere to live for two weeks at a time, and I stayed with Aljaž and Janette occasionally, in the spare room.

I've spent a great deal of my life in hotels, while on tour or working away, but making it a base for months on end is a very different experience. I had no cooking facilities. Breakfast was included – which you'd expect for over £200 a night – and I went to Wagamama's or Mildred's, the vegetarian restaurant, every single day. That was perhaps the biggest drawback. It's nice to eat out but not every night, and I was just dying to get into the kitchen and cook something I really wanted to cook.

If you're eating out all the time it can be a disaster for the waistline and, as readers of my previous books will know, I have always struggled with fluctuating weight, so I made sure I was really careful. I put on a little weight, but nothing a few high-energy performances or a season in panto wouldn't shift.

You are also very limited by what clothing you have in that situation, because I couldn't move my whole wardrobe in. I had to keep popping to Zara to buy new outfits for *Strictly* each week, which is an expensive way to live.

Needless to say, I was looking forward to moving back in and, as the weeks and months rolled on, it became clear that it was going to be a long wait. Every time I checked up, the builder told me they still weren't finished and he was still there.

In May 2017, I took them in a few beers and told them, 'We need to celebrate. It's exactly a year today that you kicked me out of my house and started work on it. And you're *still* not finished.' It was supposed to take five months.

By this time, it was habitable enough for me to live there, so I had just moved back in, but it was another two months before they finished the long snagging list. It was a long haul but it is finished now and it feels like a brand-new home. It gave me an excuse to decorate the way I wanted, because the fixtures and fittings were too new to replace before, so it wasn't worth getting anything extensive changed, like a new kitchen or bathroom. But now I have the tiles I love, the work surfaces I wanted and a beautiful kitchen.

It had been a super busy year and because I took the cruises, and holidayed more than I usually would, I didn't miss being at home too much. But when I finally got the decor I wanted and was builder-free, it was bliss.

Shortly after that I decided I no longer needed a London base because *Strictly* is broadcast from Borehamwood, and it's almost as quick for me to get to my Hampshire home as it was to get to Camden. If I'm working in London, I can stay in hotels or get a car home and Janette and Aljaž, who were set to get married in July 2017, wanted to look for a place of their own to buy.

After two decades of making happy memories, I decided to let the Camden home go. It was valued at £1.2 million – which wasn't bad considering I had bought it for £149,500 back in May 1997. In the end I sold it to a very famous celebrity who wanted it for their 23-year-old son. Lucky boy! I hope he enjoys living there as much as I did.

CHAPTER 7

More Balls and Glitter

While the builders were ripping up my home I found myself, once again, in the director's chair. *Sister Act* is a show I have always loved. I missed out on directing it at the Palladium seven years ago but in 2016 the opportunity came around again when Jamie Wilson Productions offered it to me as a touring show. Jamie is a young producer who has put on numerous shows at The Watermill as well as national touring productions. He was keen to do something different with *Sister Act* and came to me to make that happen. Together, we decided to make it actor-muso (where the actors are also playing instruments) because we thought it would be fun having nuns playing saxophones and trumpets and all sorts of other instruments.

Sister Act is a fantastic show and, in my opinion, totally underrated. Alan Menken, who wrote the music, is a genius but the show had never really had a massive outing. One of the problems with transferring a story from a film into a stage musical is that it is not easy to obtain the rights to the songs used in the film. This is what audiences come to hear so if you want to make it a hit you need someone like Alan Menken to write similar but better music and, with *Sister Act*, he did a fantastic job.

Fans of the film who go and see the stage musical invariably comment that they do miss the iconic song from the movie, 'I Will Follow Him', but despite efforts to get the rights to the song the powers that be wouldn't allow it. Personally, I think Alan Menken's songs are so much better, and the version he wrote with Bill and Cheri Steinkellner has been performed on Broadway to great acclaim, so I took that script with plans to make it into a vehicle for Alexandra Burke.

My only question casting Alexandra Burke as the outrageous aspiring lounge singer, Deloris Van Cartier, was how funny is she? Deloris has to be played by a gifted comedienne with superb comic timing who can also sing and act. I just wasn't sure whether Alexandra could be funny.

Alexandra's only stage performance to that date had been playing Rachel Marron in the musical *The Bodyguard*, which isn't a role designed to show off comic talents.

I had to be sure, so I set up a two-day workshop with Alex for two reasons. One, so I could check her comedic ability and two, so she got a taste of the rehearsal process with me at the helm.

I wanted Alex to experience my style of direction and let her see how free she can be and how bold she can be in the space without me telling her what to do. I hate it when directors command that actors, 'Do it like this.' In my opinion, it should come from the actor first – it's the director's job to mould it into something even better.

I like to improvise but, at the same time, set parameters for the actor to reach. I want the actor to create a character from their own imagination and put the colours and pictures together, to see outside their bodies.

The way I work is quite unnerving for anyone who is new to it, but it can also be very liberating. It took a day to break Alexandra down to the point where she stopped looking at and judging herself from afar. This was a warm-up for things to come and I planned to lead her towards creating the character of Deloris without her really knowing it. The process I go by involves putting the actor in the 'hot seat', meaning they sit on a chair opposite me and I interview them. They are not allowed to look me in the eye and they have to remain in character. I start with the question, 'Your name is Deloris. How do you spell that?' Then I will ask, 'Where were you born? What was your mother like? What was your father like? How did you meet your boyfriend? Did you have any other boyfriends before that?' The actor becomes the character and creates a whole backstory by filling in the blanks. Then I ask them about their aspirations and by that stage they are speaking freely as if they were that character.

It took a day for Alexandra to be comfortable with my directorial style. If I am questioning something, I tend to speak to the characters rather than the actor, such as 'Deloris, how is that possible if you were born in 1972?'

To my relief, Alex responded well and by the end of the second-day workshop she was flying, which made me feel so much more confident that she was the right fit for the show.

If I hadn't had those two days, the first rehearsal could have been stressful for her, because there is a lot to take on. You have to let your guard down as an actor and be able to be a child and foolish without feeling judged. That is hard for most people but she took to it and I thought, 'Oh, yes, this is going to be great.' Alexandra is naturally gifted, but I think she surprised even herself at how good she could be.

I came away from the workshops with better hopes for the production's future, but I confess I was still worried about whether she could deliver on the comedy brief. I thought, 'We're getting Alexandra Burke because she is a great singer and she is popular, but can she deliver a killer punchline? With only one stage credit to her name do I really want to take the risk with someone this inexperienced?'

All the other actors I had in the piece were exceptional, inventive actor/musicians who I had worked with before. They all knew how I worked and they were prepared to come up with their own ideas and concepts and different ways of looking at characters and emotions and reactions.

Alexandra had been through *The X Factor* but that doesn't really set singers up for the real world. She had been plunged into a world where she was instantly treated like a star with limos and bodyguards. She was on national television with everyone pandering to her every whim. Having won the show and subsequently released a hit single, she was pushed into stardom but to succeed in a professional theatre show she had to learn how to be exposed and vulnerable. Her inexperience was obvious at first, as she didn't know the first thing about common theatre terms such as upstage, downstage, prompt, OP (off prompt) and so on.

On the first day of rehearsals I wasn't sure how Alex would fare or whether she would remember what she had learned in our workshops. My worst fear was realized when she got up and had basically reverted to the way she was on her first day of the workshop. She had frozen up through nerves and fear, and was too self-conscious. To help her settle in, I asked Karen Mann, the free, expressive actor who was playing Mother Superior, to go through a scene with her. I was hoping this would push Alex further and show her that the rehearsal room is a safe place to explore and experiment. The scene was an argument between Mother Superior and Deloris. Mother Superior went full throttle, screaming at Deloris and throwing herself into it with a fierce energy I have come to expect from the formidable Karen Mann.

I think Alex was taken aback at how unfettered Karen's performance was, but at that moment Alex started to let go of her own insecurities and immerse herself in the character of Deloris.

She very quickly fell in love with the role and became the most gifted, comic actor we could ask for. There is no denying her natural talent but something in her was caged and needed to break out. Between myself, Karen and the rest of the company I'm so happy that we managed to release whatever it was and let her shine. It was a steep learning curve for her in those first few weeks and must have been daunting, but she picked things up quickly and then never missed a beat. My fears of working with someone inexperienced were entirely unfounded. It was actually a privilege to use my experience to steer someone who was so eager to learn and she didn't disappoint.

Initially, Alex thought the rest of the company were musicians. She had no idea that they could actually sing as well as play. I work on a show chronologically, so when I was rehearsing the nuns they had to sing out of tune as they do when they audition for the choir. Singing out of tune is the hardest thing for a brilliant singer to do, but they all managed to pull it off for the first week of rehearsal.

Then it got to the part in the play where Alex, as Deloris, is trying to teach them to sing and harmonize, and they finally get it. They started scatting and getting all Mariah Carey, sounding like total divas.

'What?!' said Alex. 'They can actually sing?' She broke down in tears when she heard their real voices, voices on a par with her own. I am not joking.

'Darling,' I said. 'Do you think I would employ people that can't sing in this particular production?' Her reaction was extraordinary. But from that moment on, her respect for the company grew even greater and she became a true company member.

Alex was also the only one who couldn't play an instrument, so she learned the glockenspiel, xylophone and percussion instruments, and she also had to learn the ukulele, which was a challenge. She became a proper ensemble member because, as I told the company, 'There are no stars in this show. It is an ensemble piece, so we all have to look out for each other.' But actor-musos are selfless performers who listen to one another with the fine-tuning attention of an orchestra, and no one person tries to overpower anyone else.

Obviously, Alexandra had the lead role and her name was putting bums on seats, although the reality of making a good show is that everyone is a small cog in a very big part of the machinery. But she was a sensation and the show got amazing reviews and was sold out in every venue for a year.

It was wonderful working with Alexandra but, of course, it came back to bite me a year later, when she signed up for *Strictly*.

*

Shortly after *Sister Act* opened, in the summer of 2016, Len Goodman announced he would be leaving *Strictly* after the next season. It was a sad moment but it came as no surprise to me. For years he had been doing both *Strictly* and the US version, *Dancing with the Stars*, and because they overlapped, that meant flying back and forth to LA every week. In 2015, he skipped *Dancing with the Stars* and only did *Strictly* but, in 2016, he did both again. That was killing him.

By the time Len decided to give up the UK show, he was 72 and dealing with constant jet lag and trying to stay awake was becoming a nightmare. He is still judging on the US show and I sympathize with that because he now goes there at the start of the series, does the gig, plays his golf and then comes home at the end. His wife, the lovely Sue, goes out there and has a long holiday with him and now he sees more of his family, so I can see why he left.

But boy, did he pick a great year to leave! The celeb dancers in that series were phenomenal. The final, between Ore Oduba, Danny Mac and Louise Redknapp, was the most amazing final we've ever seen. Every year has been amazing, but 2016 for me really stood out because of the level of talent. It was like watching a Broadway show or going to the West End and seeing amazing professionals dancing. It was highly entertaining and exactly the reason why the show is lasting so very well. But that's going to be a really hard finale to beat.

It wasn't just the great dancers that made 2016 an unforgettable year. Ed Balls' routines will be forever etched on the memory of the nation. It's not every day you see a former Shadow Chancellor of the Exchequer dancing Gangnam

Style, but that routine was brilliant and Ed Balls was so much fun. Katya Jones' choreography on that and the other routines, including The Mask Samba and the cowboy-themed Charleston, was inspired. Ed carried off each dance with such a sense of comedy that he had the nation crying with laughter.

Ed was just as much fun on tour. He has great spontaneity and a wicked sense of humour. Every night, on stage, I would judge his Gangnam dance and he would challenge me to get up and dance it myself, if I thought I could do it better. So, of course, I did, and it bought the house down every time.

Compared to most politicians, Ed seems incredibly human. He has a very clear head, he's approachable and you can understand what he's talking about because he doesn't speak in tongues, he speaks like a real human being. He can convince anyone of an argument. Actually, I want Ed Balls to be Prime Minister. He would be brilliant.

Despite being an amazing series, there were some controversies along the way. In week two Anastacia and Brendan Cole found themselves in the bottom two, with Melvin Odoom and Janette Manrara. But, sadly, Anastacia was unable to dance again that night due to injury.

In that situation, the decision is taken out of the judges' hands and it goes on the public vote. Surprisingly, that meant Melvin and Janette were out first. Janette, to me, is one of the best dancers in *Strictly*, because she is versatile. She can carry off the core repertoire of ten ballroom dances brilliantly, as well as show her strengths in a cross-section of other genres, including contemporary and commercial. Janette is a great all-rounder.

When Melvin and Janette were paired, I thought they were going to be the couple to follow, so I was sad to see them go in those circumstances. Had there been a dance-off I am convinced Melvin would have been saved by the judges, because he's such a good dancer. But what can you do? You can't force someone on if they have injury or illness. That would be cruel. If someone's in pain, there's only one thing you can do – put them on the bench.

Undoubtedly, it saved Anastacia from being first out and it was a real shock that the audience didn't vote for Melvin and Janette. But you can't rewrite history. You can talk about it, discuss it until you're blue in the face but it is what it is.

Happily, Melvin came back for the Christmas special and won, which he deserved to do because he was a good dancer.

More drama followed when Will Young stepped down for personal reasons. I thought he was doing really well, but he did look like a deer caught in the headlights. Even at the time, you could see it was hard for him. Although it is enjoyable, *Strictly* is hard work and, in my opinion, it's better to do what he did and withdraw rather than trying to press through it.

It was tough for Karen Clifton, his dance partner, and she was no doubt disappointed, but she took it in her very elegant stride. After all, the professionals still get to be involved in the rest of the series, one way or another, and if you are a professional ballroom and Latin dancer, *Strictly* is the best job there is.

Personally, I was very disappointed because I was really looking forward to seeing Will dance some more. Because it all happened so quickly, I never got a chance to say goodbye to him, which was a shame because I used to talk to him backstage and he is a truly lovely bloke. But he sent me the nicest letter, a few months later.

We were on the *Strictly* tour, in Manchester, and we

were all staying at The Lowry Hotel and, when the cast and crew retired to the bar for after-show drinks, he was there. The place was heaving with the celebrities, the dancers, the judges and the general public, and he was surrounded by people so it was impossible to say hello, plus there was no way you could have a quiet conversation, which was the sort of conversation we needed. So I just waved at him and he waved back, and that was that.

The next morning a note from Will, written in pencil on Lowry Hotel paper, was delivered to my room. He apologised that he never got to say goodbye, said he was really sorry to leave so abruptly. He said, 'I hope I didn't let anyone down, I really needed to leave the show.' He added, 'I really liked you, I enjoyed our chats together.'

He also said sorry for not saying hello at the bar that night, but it was the loveliest note and I thought it was gorgeous. He's such a love.

When he opened in *Strictly Ballroom*, in the West End, I went to see him and he was wonderful in that. And I still have his adorable note.

Presenter Naga Munchetty was always coming up to me at the bar, saying, 'Craig, why do you always have to be so awful?'

'Because your dancing's awful, darling,' I told her. 'It's not my fault. If your dancing was better, I'd be kinder, but don't you want to know what's going wrong?' I told her she was making blunders and schoolgirl errors and I said, 'I can lie to you, darling, but would you really want that? I have to pull you up on your mistakes. I can't just ignore them.'

'You could do it in a nicer way,' she said. 'You don't have to be so abrupt.'

'Yes, I do,' I said. 'Sometimes I've got ten seconds to

speak – especially if Bruno's been rabbiting on!'

The reality is that the judges get two minutes between us and if Bruno chats aimlessly for a minute and a half about dancing like hoovers and artistry, or whatever he goes on about, then I have ten seconds to speak – and I want those ten seconds to make a difference. I need to tell them what they did wrong so that they can fix it and get it right next week. Sometimes that means I have no time to add the positive. But that's the reason each of the judges takes it in turn to kick off the comments, so we all get our chance to speak for a little longer.

Lesley Joseph was incredible in that series. She is a lovely person, gorgeous to be around and for a woman of 71, she's simply extraordinary. Just like in *Annie*, she displayed an amazing amount of energy. She literally dances around like a 20-year-old. She fits everything in. She was doing *Birds of a Feather*, *Strictly*, then panto and the *Strictly* tour, so she goes from one job to the next, she doesn't stop. She is a workaholic but she loves her work like I do. I just hope I have as much energy as her at that age.

Daisy Lowe and Aljaž made such a handsome pair. Daisy was another adorable person who I really loved socializing with. Aljaž is a party animal who is always arranging parties. After the show they would all go off to Gilgamesh in Camden in the early hours, because it stayed open specially. They just loved life and loved celebrating so that was wonderful to see. Plus, after a really long, hard week of training, that's what you want to do. On Saturday night there's so much stress and when Sunday comes you get a bit of a lie-in, but then you do have to start working on the choreography and ideas and concepts for the following week's dance, so they love to let off steam after the show.

Natalie Lowe was dancing with Greg Rutherford in what was to be her last year on the show. It was sad to see her go because I loved her. She always saw the positive side of things and she's brilliant. That came out through all her years at *Strictly*, especially working with Greg, who had problems with his ankles because of his career as a long-jumper. He was so used to flexing his feet to land that he had real trouble pointing them.

On one occasion, Greg started a group dance at the judges' desk and, in between takes, we were chatting and he told me it was actually painful to point his toes. In dance, that's an essential thing, but as a long-jumper you do the opposite, so being a sportsman doesn't always help you. It can really constrict what you do because your body is so trained to do one thing, it's really difficult to train it to do something else and it really was agony for him.

'You wouldn't realize,' he told me, and he's right. I suppose it would be the reverse for me, and harder to flex my feet the whole time because I'm used to pointing them (which helps when I have to wear heels). It was interesting talking to him about that but, naturally, it didn't mean I was any kinder when it came to scoring!

When I heard that Judge Rinder had signed up for series fourteen, I was looking forward to handbags at dawn. In fact there was a bit of it, but not as bad as it was with Julian Clary, all the way back in series two. Julian has quite an evil comic tongue, which led to some great spats. While he's not so vicious, Judge Rinder still gave me a run for my money and I love that. But he is a really generous person and highly complimentary to other people. He is also fascinating to listen to as a human being and, after the show, we'd always have a laugh about what we'd said to one another. He is super intelligent and it was nice to see a real judge up there for the first time – and one with such an amazing body. When he took off his wig and gown, we saw all his rippling muscles that had been hiding underneath it all. Who knew?!

Judge Rinder brought a real sense of humour to the show, just like Ed. It was a fantastic year for that, and personalities are so important on *Strictly*. It is the celebrities that make the show, it really is, and that's what keeps it fresh and new and exciting every year. No one really knows Judge Rinder as himself, and it gives viewers a chance to see the real man. But I often watch his show because he makes me laugh. He's got the driest sense of humour and he's queen of the put-downs. He was a breath of fresh air.

To be honest, I found Claudia Fragapane and AJ's routines a bit dull. She was good, a fantastic gymnast obviously, and she had great rhythm and extension. But somehow they weren't setting the dance floor alight. She was very young and probably a little bit shy.

Then there were our three finalists – and what amazing talents they were.

Danny Mac – what a sensation! Gorgeous looking, a great body, an amazing dancer, polite, talented – you name it, he had it. His Charleston to 'Puttin' on the Ritz' at Blackpool, when he danced on the table tops, was just incredible. He was really exciting to watch and I couldn't wait to go to work every Saturday, just to see him dance.

Louise Redknapp was a fantastic dancer but everything came from an attitude of, 'Oh no, what am I doing now?' She made me laugh, but her comedy was at reverse polarities to Judge Rinder. He is the positive, high-energy pole and she's the negative, low energy, but equally as funny. I found her outlook on life was brilliant but it came from a sort of lethargy and I loved her for being open about that. Her dancing was fantastic and Kevin came up with some really fantastic routines for her.

Of course, when she split with her husband Jamie, the red-tops were all bleating on about the 'Strictly curse' again, but I don't think the show splits anyone up. Sometimes marriages or relationships are already coming to an end and maybe some people take the job in order to be separated or distracted from their problems. Strictly gave Louise a new lease of life after putting her career on the backburner to raise the kids, and that's presumably why she took the opportunity. So she could say, 'I am still here, look, I can actually do something myself.'

Being a mum is a wonderful job but some mums miss the career they had before. Your life's exciting and then suddenly you have a kid, which is also exciting, but when the kids grow up a bit, you're then free to become yourself again. That time had come for Louise.

While Danny had been amazing throughout the show, Ore Oduba went from strength to strength. I didn't really know much about Ore before, other than the fact he was a presenter, but I fell in love with him on Strictly. His American Smooth to 'Singin' in the Rain' in week three was brilliant and he followed it with an absolutely amazing jive, to 'Runaway Baby', in week four. 'This guy is incredible,' I thought. For someone who's never danced before to have that much charisma and that much style is astonishing and he thoroughly deserved to win.

Ore seems to be in everything now. He's one of the winners from Strictly that has really gone on to spectacular success because people know him and they know he's got a really good sense of humour, they know he's human. And he cries all the time.

He has a twinkle in his eye, he's got the cheek and he's got a certain *je ne sais quoi*, a proper star quality. He's someone who stands out from the crowd and what makes me sick is that he's adorable as well. You want to find something that's wrong with him but you can't. He's just a charming, wonderful man.

Last year, I got him to present the *Strictly Come Dancing Live Tour*. Every year we're looking for a new presenter, someone that's connected to the show and can give it a new lease of life. Anita Rani and Lisa Riley have both done it and Ore did it last year, which was fantastic. He's naturally gifted and, as an added bonus, I can put him into the dance routines, where he looks spectacular.

If you didn't know Len was leaving at the start of the series, it wouldn't take too long to work it out. They took the entire series to tell everyone, every week, that he'd brought out a DVD, or staging a tribute to Len, or calling a department store backdrop Goodman's and putting his name on all the bags. It was like the Len show. We couldn't get away from it. But the finale was spectacular, and a fitting send-off, after fourteen years on the show.

Len and I were and are great friends, although we never see eye to eye artistically because I'm from a different world, but that's the beauty of it. He believed that ballroom should be ballroom and that the tango should be danced to tango music, but I believe dances can be reinvented.

Three-year-olds, six-year-olds and teenagers don't want to listen to authentic tango music. They want to hear Beyoncé and Drake, and I encourage people to dance to the music that they love. I think that helps get more viewers in. Otherwise, we'd still be watching *Come Dancing* and it would only be geared to people who are aged between 70 and 90.

The music on the show is modern and that entices teenagers to watch it and makes ballroom and Latin contemporary and Charleston accessible to every age range.

I have to confess, however, I miss Len's comedy on the show. I miss his 'pickled walnuts'. I don't miss the backstage, moaning, grumpy Len Goodman but he's not always like that. He's made a personality out of complaining but he's also very, very funny and has a great sense of humour so I do miss that.

We created the show together, all those years ago, and he's taught me so much along the way. It's always hard to be the last ones standing. Now there are only four people left from the original show – me, Bruno, Tess and Anton – but *Strictly* is still going strong fourteen years on and counting, which is extraordinary.

As well as doing the American show and a regular radio slot, Len went on to front a quiz show called *Partners in Rhyme*. To be honest, I didn't think it was the best move he's ever made, and it's not my cup of tea, but I went on the show to support him and it was one of the weirdest days ever.

I had to mime a rhyme about a book and then a rhyme about a feather and they got me doing a whole host of silly things, like getting dressed up as King Henry VIII. Then there were two stagehands dressed as a horse, trotting about, for a rhyme about horses. Frankly, I didn't have a clue what was going on and it was all very odd.

Strictly will never be the same without Len and his earthy humour, and quick wit, but I wish him the best for everything he does in the future.

During the 2016 season another brilliant opportunity dropped into my lap when I was asked to teach Hugh Grant how to dance. One of the executives from the BBC was having dinner with an executive from *Paddington 2*, and it transpired they were looking for a choreographer for the film's finale. My name came up and I was asked to come in for a meeting.

They sent a car for me and I thought I was going in to meet the director and the executive producers, just for a meet and greet to see whether they liked the look of me. But when I walked into a room, I was shocked to see five people, all looking expectantly at me. I had no idea what I was going to say or do. I was going to have to wing it.

'So what do you want me to do?' I asked.

'Choreograph the finale,' said one of them.

'Okay, where is it set?'

'In a prison.'

'Have you got a photo of the prison?' I asked. They showed me a photo of the set and told me that Hugh Grant's character has been put in prison and Paddington has thrown a red sock in the wash and dyed all the prisoners' stripy convict suits bright pink.

'So,' they said. 'How do you see it?' That really put me on the spot.

'Is it a big showstopper finale?' I asked.

They said it was and asked how many cast members I would want.

'About three hundred to fill that space,' I replied. 'Do we know what the music is?'

'No, but we have an idea,' they said. 'We might want to do the "Rain on the Roof".' Luckily, that number comes from *Follies*, which I had just finished directing at the Royal Albert Hall, so it was very familiar. The panel asked if I had any other suggestions and I threw in 'Rose's Turn' from *Gypsy*. I was really making it all up as I went along. Luckily, after that ten-minute meeting, they booked me.

Hugh had to sing the number and, after discussing the choices, we settled on 'Rain on the Roof'. But the version we had wasn't right for what I had in mind, which was a big Broadway number. It didn't have any key changes, there are no builds in it, it is like a patter song between two people, but Hugh had to sing it by himself. So we decided to turn it from a duet into a solo and I commissioned a new arrangement because I wanted to put in jazz triplets and kick lines, to soup the song up a bit and make it more of a spectacle. My vision was a tap dance with umbrellas, marigold gloves, buckets and mops – and a few feather boas thrown in. All the prisoners were in outrageous pink-striped prison outfits and wearing wellies, like Paddington. Hugh would be in an open-fronted pink all-in-one with bright cerise flares.

Once we had the music in place, Hugh recorded the track and then I had to teach him to tap dance.

The first time I met Hugh, he was slightly nervous, as any non-dancer would be when the choreographer first walks in the room. He was no doubt fretting about what I had in mind and wondering if he would be able to do it.

'I would like to try it as a tap number,' I told him, after the introductions were out of the way. 'Are you up for learning a bit of tap dancing?'

'Absolutely, absolutely,' he said, still looking rather nervous. So, we went into a studio for two weeks and he trained incessantly, over and over, every single day. He spent two or three hours a day going over that one routine. Because it was Hugh Grant, of course, it was all very hush, hush and the windows of the rehearsal room had to be blacked out so people couldn't see him rehearsing.

As there were so many dancers, in different sections, I had two assistants, Michael Cotton and Ian Waller, and I put them both in the number as well. Ian was a prisoner and Michael was a prison guard, so we could have two sections of choreography and there was always someone in charge of each. The extras had to learn it in an hour, so it had to be simple, it had to be effective and Hugh had to be able to do it.

We got off to a slow start, but he really impressed me with how hard he trained. He was so diligent, persevering every single day. He was the consummate professional, very, very funny but very driven. He really beat himself up if he got it wrong, because he just wanted to do it perfectly. The language in the studio was pretty rich because every time he got it wrong there was a stream of 'Oh, dammit. Darn. Bugger it. F*** it' – and all with impeccable enunciation. It was a bit like being in the opening scene of *Four Weddings and a Funeral*. Hilarious.

Hugh has done a tiny bit of dancing in other movies, such as *Love Actually*, but he is not a trained dancer and tap dancing is a really difficult thing to learn. But he was absolutely determined and through hard work and perseverance and repetition, he got it. And he was really good by the end.

After a week he said, 'When am I going to get my tap shoes?' So we got him a pair of tap shoes to rehearse in and that really helped because he could hear the beats as he tapped.

There was one point where I wanted him to dive into a line of twenty prisoners, ten each side, and be flipped over, land on his feet on their hands then fall forward into a flat lift, being caught by other dancers. We called it the 'hurricane' lift, because that's the word he sings as he dives into the line of boys, and we created it. There's one lift in *West Side Story* that goes halfway but I added an extra massive rotation.

We tried it with the assistants first and we didn't show Hugh because if I had shown him the full lift, he would have definitely said no. It just looks too acrobatic and actually it is quite dangerous. It looks like you are an aerialist from the circus, so even when we had confirmed that it worked perfectly I refused to show Hugh.

'Show me what it is first, and I will consider it,' he said.

'It is easier, I think, if you just go into it,' I said. 'It is not a difficult lift. All you have got to remember is to hook your arms around these two dancers here and keep your body really stiff and straight, then dive into the boys.'

He practiced that bit and said, 'Oh yes, that feels alright.'

'Okay, boys,' I said to the line-up. 'We're going to do the rotation.'

'What's that?' asked Hugh, looking slightly worried.

'Just stay straight and rigid,' I reassured him. 'You don't have to worry about anything.' This time, he dived in and they all lifted his legs up and over his whole body and he did a 360-degree turn in the air and came down, but he had no idea how he had done it. The shock on his face was a picture.

'Well, that is the first part of the lift,' I said. 'For the next part you have to stand up with four boys holding your feet and lifting you up, straight-legged, and then just fall forward into their arms.'

We kept adding moves section by section and he went along with it, without realizing quite how amazing it was.

When we finally put the whole lift together it failed three times – luckily without any injury to Hugh.

'Come on, we will do it one more time,' I said. 'This time we will get it.'

He came running up, and on the word 'hurricane' he flung himself onto the boys and it all worked perfectly. It was amazing. Everyone from the extras to the producers just erupted and the applause was deafening. Hugh's face was beaming. I was filming the whole thing and when he watched it back he was over the moon, saying, 'I can do this.' He gained an enormous amount of confidence.

It's not easy for an actor to do that in front of all the extras and everybody on set as well as having to sing and do the actual tap beats himself. But Hugh refused to have a professional dancer stand in for him, which I thought was fantastic.

On the day of filming, he was as cool as a cucumber. It was the last day on set and there were 300 people in the room, all looking at Hugh. We knew we only had one day to film this entire massive Hollywood sequence because the set had to go the next day, so we couldn't do any retakes. It took a 19-hour shoot to get it right, but it looked fabulous in the end.

Being on a film set was a fantastic experience. It was great just seeing some of the other scenes being filmed, especially the animated stuff. There is no real Paddington, of course, but the other actors need an eyeline and they need to react to Paddington's actions, so there is a female actor who is the same height as the famous bear would be, and she acts all his scenes. It was fascinating to watch.

I was invited to the world premiere of the movie, in Leicester Square, but I couldn't go because I had a matinee. Mum was staying with me so I asked her if she wanted to go. 'It is the first major film that I have ever been involved in,' I said. 'I would really love you to see it at Leicester Square.'

'Oh no,' she said. 'I'll wait for it to come out on DVD and watch it at home on the telly.'

Thanks, Mum!

When she returned to Australia my sister Sue took Mum to see it. The dance was at the end, so Sue and Mum had to sit through what they called 'a kids' show' to see my moment of triumph. They actually quite enjoyed the movie but when the dance finally arrived they both missed it. Mum was too busy looking for my name on the rolling credits beside the dance and Sue was fumbling around for her phone to take a video of it and didn't make it in time. Oh well. Maybe the DVD is the best option after all.

I did get to another screening of the movie and the edit was great. The routine looked brilliant so it was worth the very long day of filming. I loved working in film. In theatre, it is never filmed, the audience will see your work once or maybe twice, but when you make a film your work is there forever, for better or worse. Little did I know, but I was soon to get my own taste of movie stardom.

CHAPTER 8

I Am What I Am

My annual trip to Australia in 2017 had an added bonus because I had been asked to do *Who Do You Think You Are?*. I had never delved too far into my family history and perhaps I wasn't that interested before, but the death of my father served as a wake-up call on many levels and made me more curious about my roots. If you don't ask your parents or grandparents about it while they are still alive, you miss out on so much important information. This was a great opportunity to learn more, so I was really keen to take part.

As I was filming for two weeks, it also meant I could extend my stay to eight weeks, which was fantastic because the show involved my family as well, so I was spending time with them while working.

It didn't feel like my usual homecoming. Usually, I would be picked up from the airport at Melbourne and would go straight to one of my siblings' houses for a family gathering. The production team wouldn't let me see the family beforehand, so the first time they saw me was with a production team and a camera as I knocked on my mum's front door. It wasn't a complete surprise as they knew I was coming and they had been prepared and briefed, but the camera crew were hoping to capture the genuine reaction from my sister Sue and Mum as they opened the door and saw me for the first time.

On the first day of filming, the car took me to the house where I grew up. When Mum and Dad separated they sectioned off the land, sold our family home, and Mum built a house for herself in the South Paddock, so the old house and the new house are next to each other. The car dropped me off at the old house, so I could walk down the street and reminisce.

'There's the wood box … I used to chop the wood and fill that up to power the wood stove,' I was saying. A few times as kids we locked ourselves out of the house and I'd have to crawl through the woodbox, which led directly to the kitchen, to open the front door to let us in. It was tricky if I had just filled the box because we would have to take the wood out first and then put it all back in. I certainly wouldn't fit through that little square gap now.

Chopping wood was the bane of my existence because that was one of the chores that the girls never had to do and I was the only boy until Trent came along. He was thirteen years younger so by the time he could wield an axe I had flown the coop and my parents had moved to places with electric ovens anyway. I pointed out the old cherry tree that we got fruit from when I was a boy, and the driveway with its slight incline, where I taught myself to roller-skate with a little help from gravity.

Walking by the old house brought back so many memories. I remembered when I was 13 and I tried to drive the car. I didn't know you had to start it in neutral so I started it in gear and drove straight into the garage door, like an idiot. My parents were not thrilled, to say the least.

While I was filming, I reflected on what it was like growing up in Ballarat, the good and the bad, and then I walked round the corner. But I didn't have long to reflect because the house Sue and Mum were waiting for me in was basically next door.

It was strange turning up at Mum's door, as if unannounced. I approached the front door and knocked loudly, hollering, 'Hellooooo.' My eldest sister Sue opened the door with Mum standing behind her, all the while the camera capturing their reaction, which I am happy to say was rapturous joy at the return of the prodigal son.

Sue was gushing in a very broad Aussie accent, 'Oh, my little bro! My long-lost brother Craigy!' and hugging me, and then Mum threw her arms around me laughing hysterically. Once we were inside, Sue turned to me and said, 'Okay, so when do we do it for real?'

'What do you mean?' said the director, Des. 'That was it.' Sue nearly keeled over because she was waiting for some sort of briefing from the production team on how to open the door and what to say. When they told her they weren't planning on doing any of that Sue's face went white.

'Oh no,' she said. 'I was really hamming it up, thinking I would get a rehearsal at least.'

Des appeased her by doing another shot but I whispered in her ear, 'You know they will go with the first one, don't you?' Sure enough, they did.

It felt quite bizarre to have our first meeting in a year in front of the camera, but it was much worse for them, because

I am used to cameras and they're not, and the lenses were right in their faces. It wasn't like the usual family reunion because people inevitably change when there's a camera around and it's hard for them to be themselves. Mum was really nervous and putting on a posh voice, which tickled me, and she was worried about the camera hitting her overhead light so kept asking them to be careful.

Sue, whose job it was to talk me through the family history and show me old photographs and documents, was equally nervous and worried about the numerous white glove documents she had to show me as her eyesight is shocking and her memory even worse.

Although it had been a while, everything in Mum's house was so familiar and nothing had changed at all. Mum is nothing like me. I am constantly buying new furniture and bits and bobs for my house, or knocking walls down and renovating, but Mum doesn't see any reason to change things on a whim or throw out something that still has its use. She will keep things until they wear out, and even then she likes to repurpose everything she can. It is a great attitude and one I wish I had, because it would save me a lot of time and money. They didn't give me the nickname Lavish for no reason! I might decide I want a Swarovski-covered overhead fan above the hotplates and who is going to stop me? But I love that Mum's house doesn't change a lot, so it is filled with all the things that make it a home, and a lot of that is our history.

Ironically, after the filming of the show Mum had an unplanned home makeover when the battery in her laptop exploded and the kitchen bench caught fire. It could have easily burnt the house down. It burnt the whole of the kitchen worktop, threw ash and soot everywhere and set some chairs on fire. The first I heard of it was an email from my sister Sue to my sister Di, which was forwarded to me.

It had some pictures of the damage attached and it read, 'Look what just happened to Mum's computer Craig gave her. She ducked out for a while and in the meantime her laptop exploded. The kitchen bench is a write off. Lucky she is not injured but it could have burnt the house down. She was so lucky.'

Apparently, it was the replacement battery that was put in, not an authorized Apple one, so it must have been faulty.

We were thankful that Mum wasn't using the laptop on her lap at the time, as that would have been a disaster. Luckily she got home just in time to save the house from total annihilation. No one was injured but it could have been much, much worse judging by the photos they sent me.

Once I was in the house and we had our meet and greet we all sat around Mum's antique dining table. Then the crew took Mum and Sue off into another room for a chat, so I couldn't hear what was going on.

'Now open the door and walk into the room,' they said. 'This is what you've got to say.'

Sue had to lead the whole interview, which is quite difficult if you're not used to it. I'm used to being in front of the camera and leading the conversation so it was odd to have my big sister taking that role, but she did brilliantly well.

Sue showed me a stack of pictures, saying, 'Do you remember when this was taken and we were sitting on the stairs with dirt all over our faces?' and so on. She produced an old black and white picture of our grandfather, Revel Horwood – who I am named after – sitting on his big penny-farthing. Then she went further back to great-grandparents and beyond and, although I had seen some of the pictures before, I had never really known who they were, so that was really interesting.

Of course, the programme also threw up some questions about my father – what sort of man he was, what our relationship was like – so I had to talk about that, which was quite difficult.

Mum was pleased to have me home on a rare visit to Ballarat but, unfortunately, it was a flying visit, so there was no time to catch up. As soon as we'd finished filming I had to get in a car to be whisked away on a tour of gravestones and memorial parks in search of the Horwood clan. I was planning to return to Ballarat after filming for some proper family time.

Mum always says, 'You never spend enough time in Ballarat,' and she is probably right. I need to factor in about three weeks though because I still have lots of cousins and aunts and uncles there as well as old friends from my early days in amateur theatre. I am patron of the local Lyric Theatre and I am also involved with the Ballarat Arts Foundation providing a regular grant to upcoming dancers.

I try to allocate four days for Ballarat out of the six weeks and then factor in my other family members. My sister Di lives in a country town forty-five minutes away called Kyneton. My other three siblings, Sue, Mel and Trent, are dotted about Melbourne and I spend a week with each if I can, with Mum bunking down at each house when she can. There are also a lot of Melbourne and Sydney friends who want to see me when I'm back so I try to fit that in, too. I also like to take a proper holiday, because I'm usually exhausted from working non-stop from August to February on *Strictly*, panto, the live tour and all the other shows and TV work in between. I might book a big beach house with five bedrooms, either locally in the Mornington Peninsular or Lorne along the Great Ocean Road, and the family tag along if they can. The weather is usually great in Victoria at that time of the year whereas weather in the northern states can be risky as it's monsoon season, but sometimes we take the risk and go to Noosa Heads in Queensland, which I love, or Coffs Harbour in New South Wales.

Six weeks sounds like a long time but it flies by so quickly.

The programme raised some absolutely fascinating stories. Although they didn't talk much about my great-great-grandfather Moses Horwood in the programme, Sue did reveal that his light-fingered antics turned out to be the reason we Horwood's ended up down under in the first place. Moses was born in 1811, in either Windsor or Oxford, they're not sure which. On 12 July 1841, he stole some cash and valuables from a hotel in Cheltenham and got caught, so he spent six months on a prison ship on the Thames before being transported to Tasmania. He was sentenced to fifteen years of hard labour, seven years of which he served.

The researchers gave me the full court report. Edited highlights follow:

Moses Horwood and James Andrews are placed at the bar charged with a robbery at the Queen's Hotel, Cheltenham on 12th of July last.

Sir Willoughby Cotton, the first witness called, said that he was staying at the hotel on the day. That he had in his sitting room a despatch box containing three orders – vis. The Grand Cross of Bath, the star and badge, The Grand Cross of the Empire and the Commander's Order of the Gulf of Hanover – a gold stamp with his line engraved thereon, two gold shirt pins in a small case and a purse containing 57 sovereigns, a £5 note and several other things. He stated that he saw all safe the night before when he went to bed at around 10 but that he missed the box a little before 8 on the following morning.

Captain Mason, Governor of the County Jail, stated that he found the box at the prisoner Andrews' house.

Mr Samuel Griffiths, proprietor of the Queen's Hotel, stated that he was informed of the burglary at 7 in the morning on the 12th of July, that prisoner Horwood had been a servant for some time in the house and was well acquainted with every part of it. He had quit his employment around five months before the burglary. Bradley Burrows, a porter in the hotel, sat up the whole of the night in question, heard a noise and footsteps and a door open in the direction of the front staircase upon which Sir Willoughby's room opened. He immediately took a candle to the front hall, heard some men whispering and then footsteps across the grass. He called out then jumped out of the back window and followed the persons. Within 3 or 4 yards of the last man they escaped over the balustrade that was six feet in height. In the garden he found a large military cloak and three hats, one of which he gave to a policeman.

He identified it as belonging to Moses Horwood, having him on Monday night at 7 o'clock in front of the hotel.

*

By coincidence, I have actually been to the Queen's Hotel in Cheltenham before. I was sent there to do a hotel review piece, and I also hold a Q&A-style 'Audience with CRH' and a Charleston Masterclass for the National Association of the Teachers of Dancing (NATD) there every two years. I had no idea there was a family connection until after my first stay, when Sue told me about Moses.

'Oh my God, I'm sure I've stayed there,' I said.

'Well, next time you go there,' she said, 'give them back the five pounds Moses stole.'

'That won't get them far now,' I laughed. I've tipped them a lot more than that in the past anyway.

After seven years of his fifteen-year sentence in Tasmania, Moses was given a 'ticket of leave' and, in 1852, he wound up in Melbourne. At that time, there was a gold rush in Ballarat and hordes of people were heading there to try to make a fortune, so he thought he'd try his luck, too.

One sad aspect of the transportation of criminals to Van Diemen's Land (as Tasmania used to be called by Europeans) back then was that many were leaving their families behind and would never see them again. According to the 1841 census, before he left England, Moses had a wife called Anne Boone and two kids, and he never saw them again after being convicted. Anne remarried in 1843, so she didn't hang around for long. Moses got married at 49 to a lady called Mary Whitton, who was from Ireland. Then he had nine kids, plus one who didn't survive, so that's not bad going. The programme didn't follow what happened to Moses after he arrived in Ballarat, but it is nice that there is still more to explore. I think he may have been a member of the Ballarat Militia group and possibly had a role in the famous Eureka Stockade Battle, that I will talk more about later. I like to think of an ancestor of mine fighting for democracy and freedom, but maybe that's just wishful thinking. I don't think he made a fortune, but he did become a miner and died at 70, on 25 March 1881, from diarrhoea, which is not a pleasant way to go.

Moses' son Charles Horwood married one Elizabeth 'Lizzie' Tinworth and she came from a very wealthy family indeed. Her parents were James Tinworth, a wealthy hotelier, and his wife Elizabeth. James' parents, my great-great-great-grandparents, were also called Charles and Elizabeth, confusingly, and they hailed from England as well.

On 19 September 1853, Charles Tinworth married Elizabeth Ann Revill in Saffron Walden, Essex – and that's where the family name Revel comes from.

At that time, British families were being encouraged to make a new life in Australia under an 'assisted immigrants' policy – much like the £10 Poms who flooded over after the Second World War – and Charles and two of his brothers, Joseph and James, decided to give it a go. They travelled by ship from Southampton to Geelong, Victoria, and arrived in May of 1854 after a three-month journey. Elizabeth was already pregnant with their first child, Mary, who was born in Geelong on 11 August that same year. They went on to have nine other children, one of whom, Charles Tinworth Jr, had a son called Revel, after his grandmother's maiden name. That seems to be when the spelling changed and when the tradition of using it as a Christian name started. My own grandad, who we called Mozza, was also named Revel to keep it in the family, and my dad was given it as a middle name, as was I. It's worked out well for me because it makes my name more interesting. When people first got to know me through *Strictly*, they thought it was double-barrelled and I still get people putting my surname down as Revel-Horwood, but Revel is my middle name and I'm proud of it.

The Tinworth family did make a fortune by mining the gold in Ballarat but their rise to riches wasn't without its setbacks.

On 24 October 1869, an article appeared in the *Ballarat Star* with the headline, 'A Chinese shot while attempting to rob a puddling machine'. A puddling machine is a contraption they used to 'puddle' for gold. It was a kind of sieve that rocked back and forth to let the water and silt through, leaving the gold behind.

Here are some extracts from the original article:

Some excitement was caused on Friday morning when it became known that a Chinese, about to rob a claim [an area of land granted to a specific company or prospector], *had been shot by James Tinworth, one of the shareholders, whose turn it was to watch the claim. The claim, worked by a party of four men only in the day time, three of whom are brothers, has been in paying ground for some time past and is known as the Perseverance Alluvial Company. Within the last few weeks gold has been several times abstracted from their puddling machine, James Tinworth saying as much as £20 worth within a week. At length it was arranged by the partners to watch the claim in turns; and a small building erected close to the shaft, and within six or seven feet from the puddling machine, served as a hiding place for the watcher.*

About one o'clock in the morning of Friday, the watch, James Tinworth, according to his own statement, perceived two Chinese coming to the puddling machine; they had no business near the claim, it being forty yards at least from any footpath, a small track for the use of the claim only leading to it. The deceased passed close to the hiding place of the watch to reach the machine, armed with a stick such as is used by Chinese in carrying vegetables, some five to six feet in length. On being challenged he attempted to escape, and the night being dark, and fearing they both would succeed in evading him, he [James] fired, and the deceased fell, the shot [No. 1] lodging in his face. He never moved, and the watch awoke his brother, who immediately started for the Ballarat East Police Station and acquainted them with the mishap.

The deceased was a very muscular man, thirty years of age, and well known to the police.

On Friday afternoon the district coroner held an inquest at the North British hotel, Plank road, to enquire into the death of Leong Mak How.

Charles Tinworth [my great-great-great-grandfather] *deposed, 'I am brother to the prisoner and reside with him. About one o'clock this morning my brother called me and said there were two men at the puddling machine, and that he had shot at them. I waited till the police came about three o'clock. No one touched the body. My brother said he first saw the Chinese coming from near the stable. The deceased went on his hands and knees to the puddling machine after crossing the whim ring. He passed very near to him, within four feet. He called to know what he did there. The deceased ran and my brother fired. I know the pistol produced, and have had it in my possession when watching.'*

Senior-constable O'Neill deposed: 'In consequence of information received, I this morning went to a claim at Dalton's Flat. On reaching there I found the deceased lying on his face, grasping the stick produced. The body was lying 62 feet from the machine – it was warm, but the hands were cold. Saw seven small wounds on the left side of the face and neck. Went to a small shed and found the pistol. The prisoner told me it was the pistol, and I cautioned him. He said they had lost within a week £20 worth of gold. On searching the body of deceased I found a piece of cloth with some matches, lottery tickets, and other trifling articles.'

Geo. T. C. Butler, M.D., deposed: 'I examined the body and found seven shot wounds on the face and neck, and a contused wound on the forehead. None of the shot had penetrated the skull, but were deeply-seated in the muscles of the face. I found much extravasated [leaked] blood at the base of the brain, at least three or four ounces. The cause of death was pressure on the brain, caused by falling on his forehead, but I could not say whether the fall was occasioned by the shot or not.'

Directed by the coroner, the jury agreed that the death had been caused by 'extravasation of blood on the brain, arising from a fall on his forehead whilst running away from the puddling-machine of the Perseverance

*Gold Mining Company, and being fired at by James
Tinworth.' It might seem obvious that being shot in
the face was the reason for the fall in the first place,
but they acquitted James of murder and manslaughter.*

Everyone went through hardships in those times and Charles
Tinworth filed for insolvency in 1865, with debts of £107
– about £8,000 today. The bill for medical attention alone,
presumably because of Elizabeth's health problems, was
£18. A small fortune in those days. It must have been really
tough but I was proud that they were what we call 'Aussie
battlers', and they refused to give up.

By the late 1860s, the surface gold that prospectors
had panned from the river was depleted and Charles and
his brothers went into mining. This time they literally
struck gold.

Charles' son Edward went into the business at a young
age and seemed to have a knack. He was 13 when he worked
out that if you found where the quartz intersected with
slate, you would find gold nuggets. That became known
as the 'indicator', and Edward found the indicator for the
Ballarat East gold field.

In June 1880, the Tinworths dug up a large nugget of 250
ounces' worth, in today's terms around $440,000 AUD or
£250,000. A year later they came across what the *Sydney
Evening News* described as an 'extraordinary find of rich
quartz' which yielded 996 ounces of pure gold, worth around
$1.6 million AUD or £910,000 today, and they continued
to rake it in after that.

We never saw any of the money, of course, because it
went to Elizabeth's five brothers, as was the custom in those

days. She was well looked after, apparently, but the boys got the money and the mining business.

When I looked at the photograph of Elizabeth and her husband, Charles, I thought, 'They're very well dressed. They look wealthy and well-to-do', but, in fact, they were relying on handouts from her brothers. If the wealth had been evenly distributed my family would have been filthy rich.

The original Tinworth's Mine, in Mount Clear, was restarted in 2011 by Castlemaine Goldfields Ltd. Today it yields around 46,000 ounces of gold a year and in its first twelve months it produced revenue of $43.4 million AUD – or £25 million – in gold revenue. Tinworth and co. would have been earning the nineteenth-century equivalent and, I'm told, they lived a very luxurious lifestyle. In total they found 30,000 ounces' worth, which in current money is over £30 million.

When I was growing up we used to visit Sovereign Hill, which is an open-air mining museum and Ballarat's biggest tourist attraction, where there is a replica of a mine. But I had never been inside a real shaft and I had no idea the extent they were still in operation. It turns out that underneath Ballarat, three miles down, it's almost all goldmines.

The *WDYTYA?* producers arranged for me to go down the mine, which was an unbelievable experience. But, I must confess, I nearly didn't get down there.

As I said, everything was kept under wraps and I had no idea what I was doing each day. The day before we went to the mines I had been to the streams where my ancestors used to pan for gold, having a go at panning myself but in the evening I was going to the opening night of *Cats* at the

Ballarat Lyric Theatre, of which I am a patron. There was a big opening night and a party afterwards and I had to make a speech so I was mingling and drinking champagne – not excessively, as I had an early start, but I had a good night and quite a late one. Then the crew turned up at 6 a.m. and took me to Ballarat East, where the gold was mined, and where my family had their own footings.

'We're going to visit a real modern-day mine and go underground,' the crew told me.

'Oh, great,' I replied, genuinely intrigued.

When we arrived at the mine there was a guide waiting at the entrance and he informed us that before we entered the mine we would have to go through a certain procedure for regulatory purposes. He told us that some members of the party would need to be breathalyzed.

The guide explained that a regulation had only just been introduced whereby your blood alcohol level has to be 0.000, so you are not allowed to have any alcohol in your bloodstream at all.

Sarcastically, I replied, 'Oh, that's wonderful because I've been out partying all night at the opening of *Cats*!'

'Not everyone has to be breathalyzed,' he explained. 'I am going to ask each of you to put your hand in this bowl of coloured balls, like a lucky dip. If you pull out a pink ball, you don't have to be breathalyzed for another week. A green ball means you don't have to be breathalyzed that day but if you pull out a blue one, your luck has run out and you have to be breathalyzed on the spot. If you blow more than zero you are not allowed down the mine.'

I broke out into a cold sweat at the thought of having to be breathalyzed, and considering I did have my last drink essentially six hours ago it would be touch and go. If they didn't let me go down the mine then it would put the filming schedule out by a day, which would be an absolute disaster. I closed my eyes as I put my hand into the bowl and felt around for a ball. Sadly there is no skill in picking out a ball of a particular colour and, of course, what colour did I pick out? You guessed it, BLUE.

So blow into the breathalyzer I did. To my horror, and the crew's, and everyone at the mine watching, my reading showed that I was a little over the zero limit. I was at about 0.3 mg/l, which is well below the driving limit, but for these purposes not completely clear.

'Have you had breakfast?' a member of the crew asked.

'No, I didn't have a chance,' I said.

'Have you got any food?' he asked.

I was beside myself, but then I had a lightbulb moment. I remembered that luckily my sister Sue had made me a chicken salad in a lunchbox. I ran to the car and scoffed it, drank two litres of water and then I had to wait an hour. Thank goodness, I blew zero when they retested me, as otherwise relations would have been slightly prickly between me and the crew for the rest of the day. They probably would have made the decision to skip the whole section about what a modern-day mine is like compared to the actual shaft that my ancestors created all those years ago, and all because I'd been to the opening night of *Cats*. But the film crew didn't know anything about the health and safety rule and if I had known I was going down the mine the next day, and was going to be breathalyzed, I would never have touched a drop the night before.

It was really interesting to see what conditions were like down the mine. It was dark, cold and clammy at the surface, but as we travelled deep into the mine, below sea level, it became really oppressively hot and humid. Newer mines are big enough to fit a semi-trailer, which is a large truck trailer, and they are well vented for air and oxygen, but even in this modern mine it was stifling, so what it was like for my ancestors is unimaginable.

The first mine they took me to was close to the surface and was the actual mine shaft my ancestors would have mined. My first impression was how small and claustrophobic it was: you literally couldn't swing a cat in there and the lack of fresh air and oxygen was most apparent. There was no natural light. Having to spend twelve hours a day in those circumstances and conditions must have been horrendous.

On the return from the old nineteenth-century mine of my forefathers, I noticed there were hundreds of spiders nesting all around the shafts. Not just any old spiders, but redback spiders!

In Australia you are taught about them at a very early age, in preschool, and as a child I was always terrified to go to the outside loo at Nana's house, as there was usually a redback lurking under the toilet seat. In fact, there is a famous Aussie song about a redback on the toilet seat. It goes something like 'I didn't see it in the dark, but boy I felt its bite'. So when I saw them at the mine I was totally freaking out.

The redback is highly venomous and is one of the few spider species that can be seriously harmful to humans. It likes to hide under outdoor furniture and bricks and is responsible for a large number of serious spider bites in Australia. Its venom is neurotoxic, meaning it attacks the nervous system and results in the syndrome of latrodectism in humans; this starts with pain around the bite site, which typically becomes severe and progresses up the bitten limb and persists for over twenty-four hours. It's sometimes accompanied by sweating in localized patches of skin and often by generalized symptoms of nausea, vomiting, rigid muscles, headache and agitation. Although not generally life-threatening, redback spider bites are capable of causing severe pain and symptoms that could continue for hours or days. Redbacks are mainly nocturnal, which worried me in the darkness of the mine shaft with only torches on our heads to see.

Those few facts show you why I was at my wits' end, trapped in a shaft metres below the surface of the earth with these monsters of the arachnid world.

So it goes without saying that I was in a little bit of a hurry to get back inside the safety of the vehicle and move on with the tour. When we emerged, we all had to be brushed down thoroughly, to make certain there wasn't a spider hiding in our equipment or clothing, or anywhere else, before we got back into the truck. I swear, for the rest of the tour I was convinced there was one lurking in my clothing just waiting to pounce.

We finished the tour of the mines without redback intrusion and I was taken to the Sovereign Hill museum to feel the weight of a gold nugget, so I could appreciate how much money that would have been worth to them. I held a 29-ounce nugget which was huge and heavy, but only a ninth the size of the 250-ounce nugget that Edward had helped the Tinworths to find.

Having seen the mines, I could only imagine how tough it was in the 40-degree heat to be toiling all day, as well as dealing with the problems of food hygiene and sanitation in nineteenth-century Ballarat. While the family was building up their empire, they were living in a tent settlement with thousands of others and raising their first three children. Diseases like dysentery spread like wildfire and there were no medical facilities. My great-great-great-grandmother struggled with health issues. She was bleeding for 37 days consecutively and was diagnosed with menorrhagia, although it could have been a miscarriage, and there were no proper hospitals. It was a real struggle for everybody but they were all hoping the rewards would finally come when they struck gold.

In 1854, before the Tinworths arrived in Ballarat, there was the aforementioned episode of the Battle of Eureka Stockade. Each prospector was allowed a plot of no more than 12 feet wide but, that year, the Victorian government imposed a 'licence fee' of 30 shillings a month for each plot – a fortune in those days – and also reserved the right to seize any nuggets they saw fit to confiscate from the prospectors by way of 'tax' on the gold. That meant they could feasibly take the biggest, most valuable nuggets of the find, if they so desired.

Not surprisingly, the miners revolted but the regional government tried to quell the rebellion by sending in 296 heavily armed soldiers. That led to a ten-minute, very bloody battle. An estimated 27 people died, mostly miners, and 113 more were arrested and tortured. They attempted to hang 13 as an example but, to the British Government's surprise, there emerged huge public support for the colonists. Despite a hugely corrupt and prejudiced trial, the jury refused to find them guilty.

Elizabeth Tinworth married Charles Horwood in 1897 and they had nine children, one of whom was my grandfather, Revel Campbell Horwood, who married Phyllis Shaw – now known as Phonse.

Because Phonse's mum, Julia Shaw, died in childbirth and her dad couldn't take care of seven children, she and her sisters were raised in an orphanage in New South Wales. She only had one picture of her mum and dad, Julia and Harry, and they looked a striking couple. She described her time in the orphanage as 'rigid and regimented', but she told me the most wonderful story.

'Christmas day was the best day of our lives,' she said. 'We got up at six a.m., as usual, and went to mass. Then we went into the dining hall for breakfast. There, on each plate, was one single sausage. Believe it or not. You could pick it up in your fingers and you could sit and eat this sausage. Wonderful.' She held no grudges. She said, 'They fed us, clothed us and educated us. What more could we want.'

Phonse's paternal grandfather, Harry Macklin Shaw, came from the cotton mill town of Ashton-under-Lyne in England. Like the Tinworths, he came over in pursuit of a better life and he settled in Glenn Innes, New South Wales. Suddenly I found myself taking a plane there, ready to find out more.

Harry Macklin Shaw, it turns out, is where I get my dancing genes from. He was a real showman like yours truly, a master of ceremonies and the only one in my family who had a bit of show business in him. My mum, Beverley, used to tread the boards in a dance troupe in her early years, and Dad and Mum could waltz beautifully, but as far as making a buck or two from performing it seemed that only Harry Macklin Shaw had followed that path. I was amazed to discover that he was the champion clog dancer of Australasia and they found a medal from 1871 to prove it. I had no idea they had competitions like that back then. Like me, he wanted to dance for a living.

He would place adverts in the *Sydney Morning Herald* which read, 'I, Harry Macklin, am open to dance any man in Australia at Hornpipe dancing for £20. Which dances the most steps, dances them the cleanest and keeps the best time.' Apparently, competitors would take him up on the challenge but they would usually lose and he would pocket the cash, and £20 back then is about $1,000 AUD today, or £560. When he wasn't hustling people as a dancer, he was working as a sheep farmer. At weekends, he would take the long and arduous journey on horseback all the way from northern New South Wales to Sydney, in search of the spotlight and to take part in dance competitions. Five generations later, I did the same when I went from Ballarat to Melbourne, towards the lure of the bright lights – although not on horseback, obviously.

Towards the end of filming, the producers set up some clog-dancing lessons, which were a scream. I met dance historian Heather Clarke, who explained that clog dancing originated in the English cotton mills. The workers wore wooden shoes because of the damp floors and, while working, they tapped out the rhythms of the factory machines. This developed into a traditional dance form.

Harry Macklin Shaw's story inspired me so much that I knew exactly what to do when BalletBoyz asked me to develop a new piece for the new touring production of *Fourteen Days*, set to open at Sadler's Wells later that same year.

I had been so moved by the story of the Eureka Stockade in Ballarat and inspired by my clog-dancing heritage that I decided to put on a show that combined those elements. I had two weeks to put on a ballet that was ten minutes long, so I decided I would retell the story of that terrible ten-minute battle, which is part of my heritage, but through clog dancing, as a nod to my great-great-grandfather. Of course, that meant I had to teach the BalletBoyz to clog dance. This was a challenge, as only one had done any sort of tap dancing and none had worn clogs. Clogs are completely different to tap shoes as they have no give in them and make your feet as heavy as lead, plus it is so painful to dance in them at first. The movement goes against everything a dancer is trained to do. The Boyz are trained in classical ballet, so we had a few minor injuries in rehearsals until they got used to them, but I could not be prouder of how brilliantly they rose to the challenge.

Filming *Who Do You Think You Are?* was like my own personal Magical Mystery Tour. I loved that I didn't know from one day to the next where I was going, or who I was meeting. Every time I turned a corner there was another huge surprise. I was told what day I was flying from the UK and I didn't know where I was going when I got to Australia at all. When they flew me to Perth, they just told me to turn up at the airport and then they told me when my flight came up on the board.

I drove around endlessly in cars, talking at the same time, which was a clever way to stop me guessing where I was going. They would just say, 'Turn left here' and 'Turn right here', so you have no idea where you're heading. The level of secrecy is quite amazing.

Luckily, everything unravelled chronologically, so I could understand the lineage and do wrap-ups at the end of the day. There was a lot of history, a lot of great stories and some really sad, tragic tales of hardship.

Perhaps the most surprising thing for me was that all my ancestors lived in Ballarat, three or four generations ago. I never dreamed for one moment that my history in Ballarat stretched so far back and I thought it had been an accident that I was born there. There is a road in the town called Tinworth Avenue, after one of my forebears, and they showed me lots of plaques commemorating my forefathers who had achieved something. Moses is buried in Ballarat cemetery, although our attempts to find the gravestone came to nothing, which was a shame.

It struck me that all my ancestors came to Ballarat from England in search of their dreams and I've done the reverse, coming from Australia to the UK to do the same thing. I'm now a British citizen and I feel like I've come home. Somehow, I never felt Australia was my true home.

It took the BBC eighteen months and £150,000 to research and produce the show and I feel incredibly lucky to have been able to take part in that programme. Not only did it bring our family together, we all found out so much about our family history and in incredible detail, information that we would otherwise never have known. It was fascinating. My only sadness was that my dad wasn't there to learn about his amazing forefathers. He would have been so proud of them and I'd have loved for him to have seen the programme.

After all that meticulous research, they got one small thing wrong – my own birth date. The family tree they presented me with at the end says I was born in 1964 and I was born in 1965. Hilarious.

CHAPTER 9

Lessons in Love

The split from Damon had led the way to some interesting liaisons but the novelty had soon worn off. It's fun for a while, but the truth is you want to wake up next to somebody, cuddle and kiss them and say 'I love you'. You want to help them get through their life as they help you get through yours, and make it better. You want someone to love, someone to care for, to live your life with and share experiences with. That's what I think I'm destined for.

With that in mind, I took a crazy leap of faith and contacted Dr Dan. Readers of my past books will be familiar with this gorgeous ex, who I had loved and lost three times already. Suffice to say, I hadn't learned my lesson and one night I thought I'd give him a ring and see how he was. We had a lovely chat and he invited me down to Bristol. It was clear the spark was still there so, naturally, we got back together.

In the past, my celebrity profile had put a major wedge between us, but this time he assured me things would be different. He said he understood that my public persona was just about work and when I'm approached in the street, there's nothing I can do to change it. I can't stop people coming up to me unless I have ten bodyguards, which would be ludicrous and, anyway, they are fans of the show and mean no malice. They're really lovely, charming people who just want to say hello and it's something I have got used to.

Over the years, I have learned to grab the iPhone or camera and take the selfies myself, so that the person I'm with isn't pressured into being the resident photographer. Nine times out of ten, the *Strictly* fan will ignore them and say, 'Craig, can I get a photo?' and then turn to my companion and say, 'Can you take the photo?' They don't always say please, either, but maybe that's because they are nervous or excited. I've had fifteen years of managing constant interruptions like that and I don't mind it, but Dr Dan found it really difficult to cope with that on the previous three times we'd been together.

When we talked about it, I tried to compare it to his work as a doctor. He has patients who will become attached because he helps them and they appreciate that.

'It's just like you walking down the street and one of your patients coming up and saying, "Thank you for changing my life."' I said. 'It's exactly the same.' Obviously, my work is not on a par with being a doctor at all, and what he does really does change people's lives. But I hope I bring a little sunshine into viewer's lives, as I know the show does.

The fourth time we got together, in the summer of 2016, he was convinced he could now cope with being the partner of a celebrity and was trying to prove it by snatching phones from people, saying, 'I'll take it.' But it became an effort on his part and it didn't feel like he was truly comfortable with it. It felt like he was persevering for the sake of our relationship.

In January 2017, Dan turned up at the house with a belated birthday and Christmas present for me. He had driven all the way from Bristol to stay for the weekend, and the first thing he said was, 'Is this working?'

'As far as I'm concerned it is,' I said, taken aback. 'We're getting to know each other a bit better. You're okay with the public thing.'

'Well, I feel like it's just going back to what it was before,' he said.

'Are you splitting up with me?' I asked.

'I don't know,' he said, looking upset.

It was obvious where it was going so I said, 'Okay, let's just call it quits now.'

He gave me his present and I opened it in awkward silence. I had a lovely weekend planned for him, which I hadn't told him about, but he said, 'Shall I leave?'

'Yes', I said and he turned and left.

If I'm honest, what I really wanted was for him to get to the car, turn around, knock on the door and say, 'I love you. I want to be with you for the rest of my life.' It didn't happen like that at all. He got in the car and he drove off, and that's the last I ever saw of him. Life is not a Hollywood movie, sadly.

So I did what I had done all the other times – blocked him from Facebook and all my other social media, blocked him from my phone and deleted his messages. I haven't heard from him since and we won't be going down that road again. It should have been three strikes and you're out but that was the fourth attempt, so it clearly isn't meant to be.

Still, I wasn't ready to give up on love yet, so I turned my attention to dating websites. As I mentioned, I had tried Match.com, but that was leading nowhere and getting boring. I went on three dates through that site and they were okay, probably because I vetted them well and truly beforehand, as I usually do. The people I met turned out to be the real deal and their photos were recent, so no catfishing. I worry about the people I meet going to the papers with every detail, so I get everyone to sign confidentiality agreements now. And I mean *everyone* in my life – from the builders to my lovers – sign them, so I have exacting working versions for employees, and more user-friendly ones for my friends. If I go on a date, I get them to sign the agreement, and if they won't do that, I won't date them. If they can't cope with that, they'll never cope with my life. It's just a bit of paper to say they won't run to the tabloids for a kiss and tell.

So far, Damon was the only one who wouldn't sign it. And look what he did – a major, untruthful, terrible kiss and tell. That sort of behaviour is ugly and I can't condone it. Now I start off on the right foot by telling people I date, 'Being with me is going to be quite public.' If I am going out in a restaurant they are going to have to get used to people coming up to me and asking me to sign autographs or take selfies, because that's what happens every single time, at every single restaurant. I'm not complaining, but it makes it difficult to have a cosy, discreet date with no interruptions. For reasons of safety, it is wise to hold first dates somewhere public. I would never invite someone I didn't know to my house or go to their house, so meeting publicly is the only way to do it, and that's not easy when you are in a popular TV show.

After three dates on Match.com I wasn't meeting the man of my dreams, so I tried Grindr but everyone on there was far too young, between 18 and 25. They're all 'twinks' – young, skinny, pretty and hairless, all looking for sex and/or a celebrity or sugar daddy. People on Grindr would ask what I was looking for and I'd say, 'A relationship,' and some of them would ask, 'What are you doing on Grindr?' I soon realized they had a point, so I gave that up.

Also, I put my full name on Grindr and several times they tried to close down my profile – for impersonating Craig Revel Horwood! I was reported by other users for pretending to be me, and using 'illegal pictures' of myself. One wrote, 'Craig Revel Horwood would never be on a dating website. In fact, I know that he already has a boyfriend, and they have two dogs and they live in the country.'

'Darling,' I replied. 'That's so last year. It is me. I am Craig Revel Horwood.' In the end, I had to post a photo of myself holding a sign reading 'I am Craig Revel Horwood'.

People are often surprised that I have put my full name up on sites like that. But I have nothing to hide and nothing to be ashamed of. If it's good enough for the person next door, it's good enough for me. Just because I'm a judge on a dance show, I don't see why I can't be a human being and live my life the way I want to live it. As long as you're not doing any nasty things on there, like trolling people, why not?

I even told everybody I was on the site when I appeared on *This Morning*. It's good advertising – everybody needed to know I'm free and I'm single, so come and meet me, baby!

I would never judge anyone who is on those sites and there are more people than you imagine on them. There's even one exclusively for celebrities to meet other celebrities. You have to pay for it, and you have to be referred by a current member and authenticated and then they set you up with other celebrities and it's all hush-hush. But that didn't work for me because I wanted to meet someone who wasn't in my business. How else was I going to meet a lawyer, a doctor, a dentist, nurse or a truck driver? I just don't meet those people. I go to a lot of red carpets and celebrity parties but everyone is so busy being their celebrity self that you don't even meet anyone in the business properly. I can't exactly go home with an A-list celeb, and even if I could, it would have to be on the quiet. I don't want to be with a celebrity, because I want to live as much of a normal life as I can, out of the spotlight.

After Match and Grindr, a friend advised me to try Scruff, because they're a bit older and have beards, which is more my type. I liked the look of it but although it's meant to be a dating site it's more of a pick-up site, in my opinion. You get asked to spend one night or even one hour with someone who happens to be a metre away. You literally switch on Grindr or Scruff and you can see which members are in close proximity to you at any given time, so it's not about finding Mr Right, it's about finding Mr Right Here!

One night, I was having dinner with some friends and I switched on my phone to see that a *very* good-looking guy was within a metre of me. I was passing the phone around the dinner table, and everyone was 'oohing' and 'aaahing' and saying, 'This guy is really hot!' And then I look up and go, 'Oh my God! He's our waiter!' He was literally standing next to us serving dinners. It was hilarious.

Ultimately, though, that wasn't the way to look for love as far as I was concerned. Anyway, I was too scared to meet with total strangers in case I got attacked or the person wasn't the one in the photo. I couldn't really relax and trust that site.

Finally, I went on Tinder, after my niece told me about her success story. She had just broken up with a guy and was with our family, visiting my grandma in Perth, Australia. She and her sister went out to a pub in Fremantle one night and her sister suggested they have some cheeky fun and go on Tinder to see who was about. Within five minutes she had connected with a half-German, half-Australian man and they fell in love. They are now married and living in Berlin, and life is a dream. So after talking to her and others, I settled on Tinder, because it seemed that was where people were looking for real and more intimate relationships. It proved to be a smart move (as you will read in Chapter 12).

Shortly after I returned from my family quest in Oz, I had a distressed call from my sister Di. She was having a personal crisis at home and needed to talk.

After an emotional conversation, it was evident to me that she was on the brink of a breakdown and just needed to get away for a while. My house in the country is a great place to relax and rejuvenate and I knew that it would be the perfect place for Di to settle for a while and take stock of her life.

'Di, you need to get away from it all,' I said. 'Come to my place for a while. It will be a change of scenery. You won't have to worry about money because you can live in the house.' I told her she could work in my office if she wanted to, or not work at all. I just wanted her to get away.

Di agreed it was time to take back control of her life so she quit her job, came over and stayed with me for five months. It really helped her because she needed a break mentally. She was ill with a shocking cold for the first two months because of the stress, I am sure. She was exhausted physically and emotionally. She needed the time to herself, which is really important.

After a few weeks of rest and recuperation Di came on a cruise with me. Mum joined us, too, as well as a couple of old friends of mine from Australia. Di had a wonderful time and came out of her shell. She met some fantastic people and the experience really boosted her self-esteem.

Di landed herself a job back in Australia before she left the UK and so, by the time she went back home, she was a rejuvenated woman with a whole new life to look forward to. I love that I am able to help my family out when they need it. I have lived overseas for over thirty years now and it's not often that I get the opportunity to be there for them. Giving Di this chance to regroup was great for her and great for both of us to get to know each other better.

CHAPTER 10

Rise and Fall

With Len gone, speculation was rife about who would be 'head judge' on the *Strictly* panel for the 2017 season.

What many viewers forget is that the title of head judge was actually invented by accident by Bruce Forsyth during a live show. He was working his way through the four of us and, in typical Brucie fashion he said, 'Now let's go to our head judge Len Goodman.'

Len was as surprised as anyone. 'Am I head judge?' he joked afterwards. 'I've been promoted by Bruce Forsyth.'

The following year it was made official, because they changed the format and added the dance-off. Because there are four judges, one had to have the casting vote if our decisions were split. So unless all three of us are unanimous, that decision lies with the head judge.

I already stood in as head judge when Len took a week off, mid-series, but I don't see that as my permanent role and I didn't want it.

In truth, I couldn't be happier with my role on *Strictly*

as it is. I earn more money from my other work than I ever would from the show anyway. I do *Strictly Come Dancing* because I love being there on a Saturday night and I get a front row seat at the best dance show on telly, so it couldn't be a better job for me. It's the best Saturday job in the world and I would never give it up, because I love it. Long may it continue. If they try to get rid of me, I won't go quietly.

To find a replacement for Len on the panel – whether as head judge or otherwise – the BBC set up auditions. I was asked to take part in the screen tests, to sit with each candidate at a desk, with the cameras lined up, judging as if it were a real show. They wanted a bit of banter, to see what it would be like to have each one on the panel and to choose someone that seemed to fit in.

I'd never realized how technical and how difficult my job was until then! It is quite strange. It's not as easy as everyone thinks, especially when you consider 12 million people are hanging on your every word and it's live. You can't go back on what you say and you need to be opinionated but you also need to have some charm and a personality that fits in with the rest. You need to be able to add something different and unique to the panel and I think that's the hardest thing.

Bruno is a very strong personality, Len is a very strong personality and I'm a very strong personality, too, but all three of us are different to one another and from completely different backgrounds. It's difficult for someone to just slot in because they can't just agree with what someone else has said. They need to know their own mind and be their own person and some people did find that hard at the audition.

When it came to Shirley Ballas' turn to do a screen test, she certainly made an entrance. She was wearing a massive ballgown with the highest heels, so she tottered up to the desk like Betty Boop. Then she leaned across and we air-kissed dramatically. She was laughing hysterically.

Every time I made my comments she would start laughing at me. I don't know if it was nerves, but she found everything I said hilarious. She was saying, 'You're hysterical, you're hysterical.'

'Darling,' I said. 'You're meant to be critiquing. You are not meant to be laughing at me.'

After that, she managed to contain herself and keep a straight face. And when she got on to the critique, I thought she was spot on and straight to the point. She knew her technical stuff to a tee. It was brilliant.

'Yes,' I thought. 'She knows exactly what she's doing and she was great.' A few weeks later it was announced that Shirley had got the job. I was pleased because I thought she was fun at the audition and we got on really well.

She was a bit worried about her broad Merseyside accent and asked if she should be more 'LA', the way she had been on *Dancing with the Stars*.

'Be yourself, darling,' I said. 'That's the whole point. Be where you are from.'

I know I don't have an Australian accent. I did, when I first arrived in Paris, but I gradually lost that after living in London for almost thirty years. I imagine that I would've maintained my accent if I had lived with fellow Australians all that time, but there's barely a trace now. Also, being involved in a lot of public speaking, as I have for the last fifteen years, means you tend to over-enunciate words so that your speech is clearer.

Of course, all the 'darlings' are just me, naturally. I'm trying to stop saying it because I have been told that some viewers have drinking games at home and every time I say 'darling' they have a slug of wine or knock back a vodka. So I guess I could be held responsible for getting the viewers hammered on a Saturday night. Next season, I'm trying not to say 'darling' too often – for the health of the nation!

Now we have done one series together, I am even more delighted they chose Shirley. I really like her and she's fitted in very well. She's a fount of knowledge, in ballroom and Latin dancing, and she knows exactly what she's talking about. If I am being super-critical I would actually say that she could be a bit *too* technical at first. Sometimes viewers at home don't understand that. You do have to speak in layman's terms for them to know what the hell you're on about, because not everyone knows what a feather step, a New Yorker or a heel lead is. You have to try to explain it in a way that everyone can understand.

If you're a real adjudicator in the competitive dance world, which she is and Len was, then you can use all the technical terms you want, because everyone understands what you're talking about. It's the jargon. Yes, the professional dancers knew what she was talking about, the judges knew what she's talking about, but the celebrities and the audience were clueless. I think she's settled in now, and knows to make her point known and understood by the audience at home. She's a really good addition to the panel and I think it's great that another woman has come on board.

The 2017 series kicked off with a shock exit, which set the tone for later surprises. When Chizzy Akudolu came bursting onto the floor, I just went, 'Oh my God, this woman is fabulous.' She was really exciting, a great dancer, with fantastic movement for such a large lady and a great personality. Yet she was booted out in the first vote.

I was genuinely shocked. In the group number in the opening show I thought she was fantastic and I was really looking forward to seeing her go week to week and strength to strength. She had a fabulous partner in Pasha and they worked well together, so it was a real shame that we didn't really get to see any of her dancing.

Then, in week seven, came the real controversy of the show when Aston Merrygold was voted out in the dance-off. Everyone blamed me because I gave his Viennese waltz a 4, and he ended up in the bottom two. But I was right and so many professionals came up to me and said, 'You know what Craig, you're actually right.' The general public were blaming me and the Aston fans were hating on me.

At the beginning of the series, I had Aston down as a favourite for the final and he was a much better dancer than Mollie, by far. But Aston got a dance that didn't suit him, while Mollie's foxtrot was a dance that she could improve on that did suit her because it was in hold. On the night, her performance was better.

It was a shock that they were both in the bottom two so early in the competition, and then we had to judge the dance-off. At that stage their previous dances come to mind, of course, and I thought, 'Aston, extremely good dancer. Mollie not so great, fudges it, and has messed it up before. Will she mess it up again?' But she came on and corrected everything she did wrong the first time around, whereas Aston came on and didn't improve at all. Out of the two, the best dance of that dance-off was Mollie's, without a doubt. So I voted to save Mollie and AJ. I will never go back on that.

Mollie King wasn't the best dancer in it but kept coming through because she worked hard. She only failed when she did Latin dances, but she was lucky. It's the luck of the draw what dance you are allocated the following week and then who you're up against in the dance-off and she got the right dances to be put through. She wasn't the best but she was resilient and I know that she was shocked that Aston went out against her because she must have known secretly that she wasn't as naturally good as him.

On the night, Mollie pulled it out the bag. Yes, Aston can dance rings around her, he's ten times better than her but unfortunately, that particular dance on that particular night was a disaster. Shame.

I hated making the decision because I wanted to see what Aston would do the following week. As a judge, I could easily have said to myself, 'Aston's the better dancer, he really should go through because last week he was amazing and next week he'll be incredible', but I wouldn't be doing my job. Bruno and Darcey voted to save Aston and Janette, but Shirley agreed with me and she had the casting vote.

I got a lot of hate for that. I was even called a racist, accused of voting for the blond, pretty one and so on. Per-lease!

It can be disgusting what people say about me, but they don't bother me. I can laugh at the abuse I get on Twitter. Everyone's entitled to their opinions and Twitter is a self-publication which is fine but, you have to remember, that

50th birthday celebrations at Fort Denison, Sydney, Australia.

ABOVE LEFT: Me and my mum Beverley.

ABOVE RIGHT: My family: Melanie, Trent, Mum, Sue, me and Di.

BOTTOM LEFT: Rietta Austin Band members: Barbara Griffin, Rietta Austin, me, Deb Collins and Fiona Leigh Jones.

BOTTOM RIGHT: My fabulous birthday cake.

My dad, Philip Revel Horwood, who was a Lieutenant in the Royal Australian Navy.

ABOVE: Here he is in New York in 1976 for the US Bicentennial, which celebrated 200 years since the US declared independence from Britain.

BELOW: Dad (on the right) in his early naval days.

ABOVE LEFT: Me at 16 on a modelling shoot – that was my old nose!

ABOVE RIGHT: Me cutting Trent's hair in our kitchen in Ballarat, 1985.

ABOVE: My wonderful partner, Jonathan.

LEFT: My new lawnmower – essential now I live in the country.

ABOVE LEFT: Len Goodman and his sparkly judge's chair.

ABOVE RIGHT: Me with Jennifer Gibney and her husband Brendan O'Carroll.

BELOW: Some of the boys of *Strictly* 2015 (left to right): Tristan MacManus, Jay McGuiness, Iwan Thomas, me and Giovanni Pernice.

ABOVE LEFT: Boy George, who performed 'Karma Chameleon' on *Strictly*.

ABOVE RIGHT: Frankie Bridge in her stunning paso doble dress.

BELOW: Lisa Riley as Dorothy in *The Wizard of Oz* and me as Maleficent for the *Strictly* Christmas Special, 2014.

ABOVE: Me and Aljaž Škorjanec having a laugh backstage.

BELOW: Me with Zoë Ball and Anneka Rice behind the scenes at *It Takes Two.*

MORE *STRICTLY* FRIENDS: The lovely Daisy Lowe (above left); Lesley Joseph (above right) who officially has more energy than me; and (below) Aljaž and Helen George who was a brilliant 2015 contestant.

Me, Darcey and Len enjoying a five-minute tea break after filming on the glass floor of the Blackpool Tower Eye.

when you post something on Twitter anyone can use that information and a lot of people seem unaware of that. They just put up absolute dross, even though they can't string two words together, and they forget that they're actually publishing a statement that can be used in a court of law. You can be sued, you can be put in prison for something you say, if it's defamation.

If anyone is being an idiot to me I will react, but not in an angry way. I wait and let the storm in the teacup finish and then I try to nail them with a comment that shows them what idiots they are.

On top of the Aston abuse, I was getting furiously trolled over Alexandra Burke. People were accusing me of favouritism because I had worked with her on *Sister Act,* and they thought I taught her to dance. What a joke!

As I replied at the time, I don't remember a paso doble in *Sister Act.* I can't remember a jive in *Sister Act*, or a quickstep. I do recall a bit of disco dancing in the show and, let's face it, the legs were hardly involved because they were all wearing habits. As if I have got time to teach her a foxtrot, when I want her doing disco-diva dances. It even says in the text, 'It is disco all the way, baby!'

I taught Alexandra to free herself, to act, to be a comic and to listen to direction. I did not teach her to dance.

From what I remember, Alexandra was quite pigeon-toed and bow-legged, because she has very muscular legs which doesn't always help in ballroom. Ideally, you need to be a bit longer and leaner in your muscle groups, so she wasn't a natural, but she was able to make choreography her own. But in *Strictly* you can't, as you have to abide by a huge set of rules from the National Association of Teachers of

Dancing, which dictate what it's meant to look like, how it's meant to be danced and it's all very – well, *strictly* adhered to. Hence the name.

When Alex started on the show I honestly didn't know if she'd stay the course, because of the tragic death of her mother, Melissa Bell, who was a wonderful singer herself.

She suffered from kidney failure and I knew she had been ill around the time that we were doing *Sister Act*, but she passed away the day before the *Strictly* red carpet launch. Alex was devastated. They were incredibly close and her mum was the light of her life and her biggest supporter. To have your mum, who you desperately love, pass away the day before you have to go in front of the cameras and pose on the red carpet is about as tough as it gets, emotionally. The glitz and glamour that is *Strictly* all becomes meaningless.

On the day of the launch, the judges attended a photoshoot for the new publicity pictures featuring our new head judge, Shirley. The celebrities also had shoots and a long day of interviews before the red-carpet event in the evening.

Darcey and Shirley were having their shots taken and Bruno and I were waiting outside the studio, before going in for the famous four shots which end up on magazine covers and the like, when Alex walked round the corner.

'Oh, Craig, can I speak to you?' she said. At that point, hardly anyone knew about her mum so I thought, 'What's this about?' But I could tell it was something serious because she's always jovial, always up and very bubbly.

Alex took me to one side, away from any prying ears and told me, 'Mum passed away last night.'

'Oh my God,' I said. 'You poor girl.' I gave her a big hug. We talked about it for a while and she said her mum was over the moon she was doing *Strictly* and would definitely want her to carry on.

'You know what you've got to achieve today, darling,' I said. 'You have to do it for your mum. Go out there and smile and wave and imagine, every time, that you are smiling and waving at her. Let it be about her. Hopefully that will help you get through it. It won't be easy,' I told her. 'It'll be heart-wrenching and I don't know how you're going to do it, but that's certainly an approach that I would take, because it's a big day for you.'

Understandably, she skipped the press interviews, because that would have meant answering endless questions about her mum and it was way too soon.

But Alex went out there, she smiled, she waved, she danced and got through that 16-hour day of filming the opening sequence, of posing for cameras, of dancing, and all with glitter flying around and everyone celebrating life. I felt so sorry for her but she was so brave. It wasn't the best start to her *Strictly* journey but she handled it with grace and courage beyond her 29 years.

There were a couple of *Strictly* 'firsts' that year, what with a Paralympian medallist and a vicar joining the line-up.

Jonnie Peacock was inspirational. He had lost a leg to meningitis when he was five and now uses a blade, and to achieve what he has in the world of sprinting is amazing. But then, to sign up to *Strictly* shows such enormous courage and determination.

I was surprised at how well he mastered all the footwork, which is intense, so I have nothing but admiration there. I made a decision that I would be as hard on him as I would anyone else, because that's what he would want, so I did pick him up when his blade leg was out of time during the jive.

He was a great sport and such a driven and talented sportsman. He also created awareness that disabilities can be overcome. His triumphs are a great way to give people that are in the same predicament a new lease of life and to show them what great heights they are capable of achieving.

We had our first clergyman in the shape of the Reverend Richard Coles. That was brilliant casting because it meant he could do godly routines, arriving on a cloud coming down from the heavens in week one, to the tune of 'There Must Be An Angel', and dancing around in a sparkly dog collar.

He's barking mad, which is great, and openly gay, with a husband. Imagine being a contestant like that on *Come Dancing* thirty years ago. Everyone would have been shocked. It's a wonderful indication of how far we've come that he is totally accepted and can say, 'Yes, I have a husband and I believe in God.' Sometimes clergymen seem otherly, because they're done up in that regalia all the time and you don't always think of them as people with emotions, but watching him get up and take a stab at the dancing showed how human a reverend can be.

With Richard, you could speak about anything you wanted and you didn't have to mind your Ps and Qs. Of course, he was a member of The Communards so he had enjoyed a career in the music industry, but he had never danced properly in that role. He was just completely down to earth, completely normal, cracking jokes all the time and he was in there for a laugh. He didn't have any delusions of grandeur, and he knew his dancing was far from heavenly, but he was great and he brought something different for people who are spiritual and Christian.

We had a plethora of funny contestants that year, with the Rev, Brian Conley and Susan Calman.

I had worked with Brian in 2011 on a touring production of *Brother Love's Travelling Salvation Show*, which is a Neil Diamond tribute show. Brian played the older Neil Diamond, Darren Day played the middle-age Neil Diamond and Ben James-Ellis played the younger Neil Diamond. Brian was wonderful to work with. Really inventive and creative, and we got on like a house on fire. It was great to see him in the show because he went off the map for a bit and this got him back on TV and introduced him to a brand-new audience. *Strictly* is watched by 3- to 93-year-olds so many of the younger ones were getting to know him for the first time.

Brian's brother Alan has been a floor manager on the show for fourteen years and we've talked about Brian, so it was great to see them working together and exchanging a bit of brotherly banter. Alan's also a great guy and a first-rate floor manager.

The other contestant providing the laughs was Susan Calman. She was taking herself a bit too seriously to begin with but, about halfway through, she started getting into it and understanding the programme, and then she did her fantastic Wonder Woman routine. Technically it was terrible, but who cares? It was entertaining, it was enlightening and she really brought some wonderful Scottish humour to the whole proceedings, so viewers in Scotland were voting for her. That and her superhero powers took her a remarkably long way.

Charlotte Hawkins was a bit of mystery. She's tall and elegant and looks like she would be great on the dance floor, but she was clumsy.

Simon Rimmer was great. He knew his limits and his talent and he was always putting himself down, and I secretly liked that. The day after the show, I would always watch his programme *Sunday Brunch* to see what he was talking about and he would say, 'I'm a terrible dancer.' Actually, he wasn't as bad as he thought he was. He was self-deprecating, but he saw the funny side and made a joke out of it, so I really liked him.

The nation adores Ruth Langsford and I can absolutely see why. What you see is what you get, and she is every bit as lovely off camera as she is on. She was terrified but I also think she thought she'd be better than she was. Her husband, Eamonn Holmes, was making me howl with laughter because he came up to me in the bar and said, 'Craig, you were absolutely right about Ruth. She's terrible!' I couldn't believe it. I thought to myself, 'At least she has her husband to pick up the pieces after a bad night,' but he was saying, 'She should never have done it. She's terrible.' But that's Eamonn's sense of humour, and part of the banter between them that viewers love.

Ruth tried hard, though, and I can only encourage that. I wouldn't put her down for the sake of putting her down but I did have to tell her that it was all a bit pedestrian, often out of time, and some of the lines weren't quite right. It didn't all gel together well, even though she might have felt like it did.

It's not uncommon for celebrities to think they've done an amazing job and nailed it on the night. But when you are judging it, it's the only time you've seen it in its entirety, so I can only judge what I see in that ninety seconds. Ruth took it in good humour and, in the bar, she would come and sit with me and say, 'Can you be a bit kinder towards me?' She was so cute.

I was so pleased that she was like she was on the telly. In contrast, in real life I am not anything like I am on the telly, because I am not judging. If I'm on *It Takes Two*, people see the real me, but not on *Strictly*. Everyone does think I'm going to be quite nasty in real life but I am actually really lovely and beautiful and delicious and loving and all-embracing and generous and sweet. Honest! But just put a bad dancer in front of me and I turn evil.

Davood Ghadami was fantastic, and gorgeous to look at. The rippling muscles on that body were really distracting, but he did such a great job with Nadiya Bychkova. They looked incredible together and he danced extremely well for someone who had never moved that way before. He was quite stiff to begin with, but he ended up developing an artistic style which I really appreciated and he worked very hard to achieve that.

Everyone had a bit of trouble pronouncing his name because when you see it you want to pronounce it 'Dav-ood', with double 'o'. But it actually rhymes with 'Harvard', so we all had to practise saying it that way.

The finale, with Gemma Atkinson, Alexandra Burke, Debbie McGee and Joe McFadden was fantastic. Aljaž came up with great material for Gemma. She's very fit and loves pumping iron but her physique worked really well in the paso doble, and she became elongated and elegant within the ballroom as well. She trained a lot, took it seriously and pushed herself really, really hard.

Gemma wasn't as naturally gifted as Alex, Debbie and Joe, so she was in a difficult group. Everyone mocked me when I bowed down at the feet of Debbie McGee, but she was extraordinary. What a woman! I don't know what possessed me to do that and everyone was calling me 'cheesy' but, as I said, sometimes the other judges overrun so I don't even get to speak, so I thought 'actions speak louder than words'. I think she's incredible and yes, I'll kneel at her feet to prove it.

We do that in the theatre all the time. If a total star walks into the room, such as Bette Midler, I am on my knees. It's a gesture that can't be bettered. Yeah, it's cheesy, but so is the show. So what?

Debbie turned 59 in the course of the series and she danced like a 20-year-old. She was so nimble, so precise. Yes, she'd had some classical ballet training, but she hadn't danced like that since she was 23 and to dance the way she did at her age was extraordinary. Plus, she had to learn all the ballroom stuff, which is always difficult for ballerinas. When Darcey trained in ballroom she found it really difficult because, in ballet, your hips and feet are turned out, but here you have to turn your hips and feet parallel, and that's so unnatural for a ballerina. I would liken it to Greg Rutherford having to point his feet instead of flexing them. Once you've been trained in something it's really hard to undo it and learn completely new habits, but Debbie did. She put every bit of energy and every bit of thought and then every bit of herself into it.

It was so good for Debbie to perform as Debbie McGee and be known for more than being Paul Daniels' sidekick. She's lost her husband, the person that she loved all her life, and they had a wonderful life together, but she had always been known as a magician's assistant. I was so glad for her that everyone finally knew her as Debbie McGee.

She had a really strong following and she totally deserved to be in that final.

It was great to see Alex getting through, especially after the death of her mum. Lisa Riley went through a very similar experience because her mum died just before the show and never got to see her take part. It made her a stronger person in the end, but she only got to grieve properly afterwards. I wrote the show called *Strictly Confidential* for Lisa specifically to star in, to tell her life story through dance, and we talked a lot about her mum and that also helped her get over it. *Strictly* is all encompassing and very absorbing and it's difficult to grieve through that process, through those four months. So it probably hit Alex hard when she finished the final and had a couple of weeks off before the tour.

If you make it all the way to the final, you are 'Strictlified' for four months of your life. Unlike a prison sentence, you get fed beautifully and you get to dance with amazing people, in gorgeous costumes, but you are locked in to rehearsals, studio time, VTs, interviews and so on, and you can't escape it. It's difficult. I don't think viewers always appreciate just how exhausting getting to the final can be. At that point, the interviews become incessant and the VTs go down to four people, so the entertainment is not spread about the entire company anymore. The focus is primarily on the finalists so you have to have stamina, and Alex did amazingly well.

Joe was absolutely amazing and could do things that no one ever thought he could do. His Viennese waltz with Katya told the most immaculate story and was so full of character and drama. I loved it. I think he and Katya did a great job and totally deserved to win, but then I would say that the three of them, Alexandra, Debbie and Joe all deserved the trophy.

Before the final, I would rate them as the top three and Gemma as the runner-up, but if I was being super-honest, I would put Joe third, Alexandra second and Debbie first. My opinion doesn't matter now, but I thought Debbie was spot-on and extraordinary, and that Alex had more power than Joe. But the audience decided that Joe was the best man to win, so congratulations to him.

All four finalists came on tour and it was one of my favourites, because the cast were great. The presenter was Ore and we had a Hollywood setting with big gold palm trees, flashing cameras and red carpets. It was so showbiz and glamorous – right up my alley.

The cast got on really well. They were just a really gorgeous company who loved the live audiences' reactions, because you don't get that in TV. When you go out on the stage of the arena and there's 15,000 people shouting your name, you truly know the power of *Strictly Come Dancing*.

Although we didn't know it at the time, series fifteen turned out to be the last one for Brendan Cole. Brendan has his live shows, which is fantastic, and he had already signed up to play Prince Charming in panto, so he was moving on, and that is all you can do. We've had our run-ins in the past, some of them on screen, especially when we were both judges on New Zealand's *Dancing with the Stars*, but he is extremely talented. The talent just has to be used in a different form from now on. I told him I would consider writing a one-man show for him, because I am all for ending one career and starting a new one and this is the perfect time to do it.

I know how it feels when you have to take a new direction in life, believe me. It's scary. When Cameron Mackintosh sacked me from *The Witches of Eastwick*, I was literally thrown out of the double doors into the dance gutter. The most I could earn that year was £9,000, and I couldn't pay my mortgage. I had to give up my mobile phone because I couldn't afford it. But I had to pick myself up and get on with it, and that's when I became a choreographer.

You have to take a different tack in life sometimes. It is like a baby bird being pushed out the nest to see if it can fly. You fly or die. I wish Brendan all the luck in the world.

CHAPTER 11

A Day in The Life of a Drag Queen

When *Annie* was scheduled to open in the West End in June 2017, Miranda Hart stepped into my high-heeled shoes and took on the role of Miss Hannigan. I'm always booked a year in advance and I was too busy at the time, but Miranda was an interesting choice. She's a great comedian and a softer Hannigan than me, but would be funny to watch.

At the time, I did feel a bit sad that I wasn't returning to the role, partly because Miranda's West End *Annie* opened at one of my favourite venues, the Piccadilly Theatre, where I choreographed *My One and Only* and also my first West End show as a choreographer: *Spend, Spend, Spend*. That place holds a lot of memories for me and posters of the shows that I choreographed are hung up backstage.

Little did I know, however, that the formidable Miss

Hannigan was about to come back into my life. Miranda's contract was coming to an end in September, so they rang and asked if I could take over for ten weeks.

It wasn't great timing. It clashed with *Strictly* and would take me right up to panto in Southampton, where I was playing the Wicked Queen in *Snow White and the Seven Dwarves*. I had toured that show for five years all around the country, but this time it was a completely new script and there was a lot more comedy, a lot more dame material that I don't normally do, so there was a lot to learn. Plus I was voicing 52 episodes of a new Disney animation *Sadie Sparks* at the same time.

Sadie Sparks is a magical animated children's TV show, which will air on the Disney Channel in 2019. It follows the enchanting story of a 14-year-old girl, Sadie, who finds out she has magical abilities and becomes a wizard-in-training. She comes under the guidance and mentorship of a very old and very grumpy rabbit, Gilbert, who is sent to the human world from the magical realm to train Sadie and harness her volatile magical skills.

I voice the character of Cornelius – a charming but snobbish and snidey snake, who mentors Sadie's nemesis, Blaine. Cornelius is a morally dubious snake who is a bad influence on Blaine and all those around him, so he couldn't be further from my own persona. I really had to get into the mindset of that character!

Working on this brand-new animated series has been a lot of fun. I can't wait for the audience's response to the colourful collection of characters. I had the opportunity to work with a stellar cast, including young British talents Georgia Lock and Sammy Moore (previously in the Disney Channel show

Evermoor Chronicles), and the comedian Rufus Hound, who incidentally won the 2013 *Strictly* Christmas special and was crowned King of the Christmas Ballroom after dancing a tango with partner Flavia Cacace. The pair scored 38 points from the judges for their routine to 'Never do a Tango with an Eskimo'. Rufus said his experience on the one-off show was 'surreal in the extreme'. Well, that's exactly how I felt about my experience of voicing the role of Cornelius.

Other cast members of *Sadie Sparks* are Tyger Drew-Honey, Dominique Moore, Morwenna Banks, Laura Aikman, Dan Renton Skinner and Rufus Jones. The series was created with kids aged 6 to 12 in mind, but it really does have something for everyone. It is the perfect show for kids to watch together with their parents and the rest of the family – just like *Strictly*.

In spite of my packed schedule, the offer to star in *Annie* at the Piccadilly was like going home. I couldn't say no.

It was a busy time and I was putting pressure on myself to do everything. I admit I was doing too much, but I was also enjoying it.

To make matters worse, my left hip was giving me hell. I had surgery on my right hip in 2013, but the years of dancing had finally caught up with the other side and I was in agony. I had known that the operation would be necessary a year earlier, but my doctor advised that it wasn't far enough gone. I knew that it was going that way and as I was in a lot of pain I very much wanted it seen to, so while there was a gap in the diary, in February 2017, I went to see the doctor. I demanded an X-ray.

'It's just not really ready to be operated on yet,' he told me. 'It's not bad enough.' I knew it needed to be done and he agreed that, eventually, it would, but he explained that he didn't want to take bone away just for the sake of it.

'Fine,' I thought. 'I can cope with it.' *Strictly* wouldn't be an issue and as long as I could get through panto later in the year, I thought I'd be alright. But then I was offered the part of Miss Hannigan in *Annie*, and that meant a lot of dancing.

I went back to the doctor and asked, 'What can I do?' He put me on a pain management schedule for eight months, which involved taking painkillers two hours before I had to dance, so they would kick in at the right time. They were only over-the-counter tablets, paracetamol and ibuprofen, but I imagine they're not good for your tummy and I didn't want to spend a year on painkillers.

Even so, *Annie* in the West End for me was a dream come true – and I knew it would be a dream come true for Mum, so I secretly made arrangements for her to see it. My sister Sue and her husband David had planned a trip to the UK and, quite by chance, would be there on the opening night. It's always special if a family member from Australia can come and see one of my shows as it doesn't happen that often.

Having accepted the role, though, my schedule from September to Christmas was manic.

Although I am only in the studio for one day a week, *Strictly* isn't just a Saturday job. I have to go on and do *It Takes Two*, press interviews and photoshoots, which means getting dressed up, made up, having your hair done and so on. Believe it or not, it takes four hours to get one photo, or a whole day if it's the cover shoot, as well as factoring in the travel time to get to London. Then the interview to go with the photograph takes a while as well. I had long days fulfilling all sorts of *Strictly* commitments, then I would go off to do *Annie* in the evening. I was doing a full-time job, as well as performing at night.

To top it all, in the early mornings I was learning my panto script, because that was the only time my brain was functioning well enough to absorb the lines. By the time I got home from *Annie* late in the evenings, I was exhausted. I had no time to party, no time to go out for dinner.

Because I had sold my house in Camden Town, I rented a flat just around the corner for three months. I knew the area so well that I felt at home. That worked well, because I was in London for all the other work, and could get to and from *Strictly* without a hassle.

Within my crazy schedule I had to build time, every day, to become a woman – with all the preening and primping that required.

A day in the life of Miss Hannigan:

07:00–09:30
Learn panto lines and reply to the usual daily emails, etc.

09:30–10:00
Breakfast

10:00–10:30
Shaving – but not the face.

I get in the shower and shave my body hair. I start with my armpits and then remove my chest hair, because Miss Hannigan wears a dress with a plunging neckline.

All the time I am showering, I am gently warming up my voice, because I have to sing high notes and warming up helps to prevent damage to your vocal chords. I would be humming in the shower to make sure I had a voice for the performance that night and to gently get my whole body going.

The next thing I do is pluck my eyebrows, because they can't be too bushy and I need to make sure there are no stray hairs in between, because you can't cover up the centre with brow wax (see below).

10:30–12:00
Telephone interviews for *Annie, Strictly* and panto.

12:00–13:00
Test what I've remembered from the morning line-learning session and recap if necessary.

13:00–14:00
Lunch.

14:00–16:00
In between my other jobs, I often have to get my nails done. I wear acrylics and I have to get them fixed with gel fillers, but the nail polish has to come off after each show, so we redo them every day. The acrylics are quite long and have to stay on the whole time – even when I was on *Strictly*, which didn't go unnoticed. Viewers began tweeting about them and asking, 'Why are Craig's nails so long? They look ridiculous.'

16:00

Car to theatre.

The visit to the nail store takes an hour and a half and then I arrive at the theatre, go straight to the dressing room, collect mail, sign all the photographs I have to send off and get any paperwork done. There's often fan mail which you have to reply to, so I always allow around an hour for that. I generally have to do interviews when I am at the theatre, too, so they would happen either before I start dragging up or, occasionally, during.

Admin done, I start the process of the make-up, which includes my eyes. To cover up my eyebrows, I use this semi-solid wax which you put between your fingers to warm it up until it is the consistency of plasticine, and then smear on your eyebrow. Then you add a solidifier and that takes seven minutes to dry.

While the solidifier is drying, I have a close shave. I have to shave 'up', against the grain of the hair, because my facial hair grows quite fast. On a two-show day, the beard starts coming through for the evening show, which is not a good look. I shave down first, and then I go upwards, because it has to be really close. Not many women know this, but shaving up really hurts. It's not a pleasant experience.

By the time I've shaved, the eyebrows are dry. So, I put on the base, meaning I apply a thick foundation on top of the wax that is covering my eyebrows. That is then powdered down.

Next, I apply a proper base, over the top of the initial one. That has to cover my face, neck, chest and shoulders so that they are all one colour, otherwise you end up with a red neck, a white chest and a brown face. So, I had to do my whole neck, right down to my boob line.

The eyebrows go on after that. It is 1930s make-up, so the brow line is quite extended and long, and it's quite hard to achieve. I use a fine brow pencil for that.

Once the eyebrows are done, I put the eyes in place. First, I put glue onto the false eyelashes, because you need to wait for three minutes before they stick to your eyelids. If you make the mistake of putting it on too early, they slide around everywhere and glue your eyes together. If you make the mistake of leaving it too long, they won't stick at all, and then you have got to take them back off and start again. While I wait, I put charcoal all around the eyes.

Once the eyelashes are on I start blending, then I put lipstick on my lips, rouge my cheeks and put mascara on the bottom lashes, rounding it all off and finishing the face.

Before I paint my fingernails, I change out of my robe and into a tracksuit and trainers for the company warm-up, because that is compulsory.

My nails need to be dry before I can do any extra work on the make-up, or put the wig or the dress on. We all know how long it takes nails to dry. So, I put on the first coat of nail varnish then patiently wait, fanning them and using a special spray that helps them dry quickly. Then I do a second coat, because the first coat never looks good enough.

As the nails are drying, I go downstairs to do the workout session and warm-up sessions, which last twenty minutes. Theatre people are quite demonstrative and tactile, so at the beginning of the run I had to stop people coming up, saying 'hi' and hugging me, because my nails were still drying. But they soon got used to my routine.

You can imagine how I look in a bloke's tracksuit with a full face of make-up, false eyelashes and painted nails, but the company got used to that, too. In fact, no one ever saw me as Craig, because I was the first one in and the last one to leave. On one occasion, I was running really late and I came down without my make-up and everyone said, 'Oh my God, you've got no make-up on.' They are so used to just seeing me turn up with a full face on, and my nails done.

Warm-up over, it was time for the tights. First, I would do the tuck job to get rid of my boy's bits. It's not as uncomfortable as you might think. You pop your testicles back up into their socket and pull your willy towards your bum, put the G-string on and a pair of tights. I use the thick, opaque and skin-coloured Capezio show tights that female dancers wear. They are thick enough to cover up my leg hair because I didn't want to shave my legs. On top of all that goes a pair of show knickers, so that when I kick my legs, people can't see anything. I wear a pair of black M&S Spanx-type control knickers.

Next, I put on the Hannigan 1930s stockings which are all wrinkled, because the legs have to look haggard and trollopy, and the stockings need to look like they have lost their elasticity. Then the shoes go on. For panto, I wear four to six inch heels but Hannigan's are only two inches, because, as I said, it is the 1930s.

Fifteen minutes before curtain up

At this point I am sitting in my robe with the tights, stockings and shoes on, because once I have got the corset on, I can't bend over to do the buckles up. At the fifteen-minute call, I am dressed and prepped and ready – all apart from the corset, dress and wig. The corset has to wait until the last minute because once I am strapped in, I can't get out of it to use the toilet for the whole show. I always have to remind myself to go to the loo even if I don't need to, because there is no possible way of going to the loo in between.

Then the dresser comes in, puts the corset on and, because I can't bend down, they clip my suspenders onto my stockings. With the corset on, the boobs have to go inside and the mic packs have to go into the boobs.

They use prosthetic ones that move more convincingly when I shimmy, and they have proper nipples so you can see a bit of an outline of them through the bra.

Two microphone packs are then placed into the back of the boobs, towards my skin with one behind each breast. With no way of changing a pack if it fails, they need to have a backup, which is why I double up. The mic is then put on my head.

Ten minutes before curtain up

When the laces are pulled tight and I'm all cinched in, having achieved the body of Hannigan, I sit back down and the stylist comes in to put the wig on. The wig is pinned into pin curls that have been prepped earlier with a wig cap, and then the lace around the hairline of the wig is glued onto your face.

Five minutes before curtain up

Next, I get into my camisole, the lingerie Hannigan is so famous for. Then the watch, the jewellery, the earrings, the whistle, the keys and all paraphernalia is added and we get 'beginner's call', which means I have to clippity-clop my way down the stairs, collect my gin bottle and I am ready for action.

It is a long preparation to come on for nineteen minutes!

One crazy story happened while my sister Sue was visiting. Just after opening night, we went to the pub next to the theatre in Piccadilly. While I was outside chatting on the phone, a down-and-out drug addict stole my backpack from right under Sue's nose. The crafty joker somehow managed to snatch it without her seeing. Once we realized it had gone, we ran around Piccadilly looking for it, to no avail. I had my wallet in the backpack which had quite a bit of cash and I also had a set of beautiful royal coffee mugs from the Palace, given to me by Prince Andrew, no less. I had planned to gift them to my mum, so I was very upset about them going missing.

The following day, the police came to the theatre to interview me. They turned up right at the time I was prepping to become Miss Hannigan. They must have thought it was one of those crazy days on the beat, because at the start of the interview I was Craig Revel Horwood and by the end of it I had completely transformed into Miss Hannigan.

The two officers were mesmerized as I donned the make-up and eyelashes, but acted as if it was just any other police interview. They located my backpack the next day, at McDonald's around the corner, minus the money in the wallet. Sadly, he had also taken my royal mugs, which was the one thing I thought was irreplaceable. However, my trusty PA Clare made a call to the Palace and they were nice enough to replace them, so now they have pride of place in my mum's home.

Mum was still keen to come and see me starring in *Annie*, so I booked for her and Di's daughter, my niece Aleisha, to come over for a holiday. Mum had visited a couple of months before, so she had two long-haul trips in one year, but she thought it was worth it to see her son on the West End stage. With my crazy schedule, I didn't have much time to spend with them, and when I did they had to help me with learning the lines for *Snow White and the Seven Dwarves*. My niece Izzi popped over as well, and being a trained actor she was keen to help me run lines, too.

There were so many lines to learn that were totally new, plus different songs, or the same songs with completely different lyrics. It was difficult retaining it all while still playing Hannigan, because I had two major scripts in my head. It's a wonder I didn't start spouting 'Mirror, mirror on the wall …' in the midst of a drunken Hannigan scene!

As soon as the West End run was over, I went straight into panto. I finished *Annie* on Friday night, did *Strictly* on the Saturday, had Sunday off and started panto on Monday.

This panto was bigger, better and bolder than the previous ones I had taken part in. The costumes were more exaggerated and the sets were enormous because we were in the Mayflower in Southampton, which is a huge barn of a place with a 2,300-seat capacity.

I had all new costumes, and six-inch heels to deal with,

which is frightening, and to make matters worse I was suffering acute pain in my hip and I was on painkillers the whole time. It was a real challenge but, of course, you can't back out of these things because your name is advertised and you don't want to let anyone down. You've got to get through them in one way, shape or form. I adapted the choreography to suit my body a little better, so I could get through it, but two shows a day was exhausting and painful.

The Chuckle Brothers were also starring in the show, as Queen Lucretia's henchmen, which was great. Initially I thought they could be a bit old-fashioned, but they were brilliant. They brought the house down every night. People love them and they were great fun backstage. I was so sad when I heard that Barry had passed away. He was a legend.

The dance troupe, Flawless, were also in the show and gave it a really modern twist.

I have to confess that when we opened the panto in Southampton it is probably the most nervous I have ever been. I felt totally under-rehearsed because I still had *Annie* in my head, I had *Strictly* going on, all the spin-offs from *Strictly* and the voice work for *Sadie Sparks*. Also, I wasn't used to stand-up and there were a lot of one-liners, political jokes, topical jokes and things that I don't normally do as the queen, so that was challenging.

In my nervous state before the first night, I couldn't help casting my mind back to 2009, when I had played the role of Lucretia for the first time and received the worst review I'd ever had. It was my panto debut, in Llandudno, and Michael Thornton, writing in the *Daily Mail*, savaged me with a scathing attack that puts my *Strictly* critiques in the shade.

Referring to me as an 'Australian-born, former rent boy, small-time drag queen and former chorus dancer', he recalled Julian Clary calling me a 'silly old queen' and said I was now playing one on stage. He went on to call me 'ugly' and wrote, 'Now removed from the cover of his Saturday night *Strictly Come Dancing* desk, Horwood is revealed to have a paunch and excess weight on his rear, a fact that not even his lavish costumes can entirely conceal.'

He said I had no discernible acting skills and went on, 'His singing was inaudible. For a choreographer, he moves badly, with arm and hand movements that resemble an octopus with St Vitus' Dance. And his hoofing, in one brief costume that revealed more than it was wise to show, looked as laboured as a 60-year-old woman with varicose veins.'

Charming!

I honestly don't mind bad reviews because I think you can learn from them. I must say, I did laugh at that one because, although it was brutal, it was eloquent. It was also quite notable for being more acerbic and cutting than I have ever been on *Strictly*. Even I wouldn't stoop so low as to point out people's paunches and chubby rear ends!

By the second week I had got into my stride, but the first week was terrifying, every day. I had three scripts placed about the theatre. I had one script with my lines highlighted in bold on stage left, one script on stage right and one script stuck up on the mirrors in my dressing room. It was so wordy and every time I came off for a quick change, I'd have to revise the script for the next scene.

To my relief, the show went really well and the reviews were fantastic.

As an added bonus, I could live at my house, because it's so close to Southampton. That meant I could actually spend Christmas day at home – for the first time in eight years. I spent it that year with my Australian ex-girlfriend, Dee (who I wrote about in my first book *All Balls and Glitter*), her husband Rob and their lovely family. It was like a proper Aussie Christmas in Hampshire, minus the sun-drenched weather, of course. So wonderful to be at home with great friends, however short-lived.

After Christmas, there was little respite from the relentless schedule either. I finished the panto run on 7 January, which was a Sunday, with two shows. On Monday morning at 9 a.m., I had to be at rehearsals in London for the *Strictly Come Dancing Live Tour*. It didn't stop. By the time the tour ended I had literally worked seven days a week for six months. It was exhausting both mentally and physically, but I knew that there was time off coming up with my usual six-week break in February, so I resolved to push through it.

When February came, however, my non-stop schedule and the dancing had taken its toll on my body and had made the pain in my hip unbearable. Having danced in *Annie*, got through the panto in six-inch heels and then danced on the *Strictly* tour, I knew something had to be done if I was going to keep working and performing.

Instead of my usual trip to Australia in February, I planned to book time off to have the hip replacement and then recuperate in peace.

But, before I had a chance to go under the knife, another once-in-a-lifetime opportunity came along. I was offered my first lead role in a movie, *Nativity Rocks!*

It has been one of my life's ambitions to be in a terrible B-grade horror film, like *The Blob* or *The Lair of the White Worm*, that becomes cult viewing. This was no B-movie, obviously, but it was the closest thing I was going to get because I would be playing an evil queen who is horrible to everyone, including children.

I just couldn't say no. The hip would have to wait another six weeks.

CHAPTER 12

From Rock Opera To Hip Op

My big screen debut came about by chance. My wonderful assistant choreographer, David James Hulston, was working with writer and director Debbie Isitt on *Nativity*, the stage musical, as was another friend, *Annie*'s musical director George Dyer, who was providing the arrangements for the score. I was invited to the opening night at Birmingham Rep in October 2017, because there was a role in the show that the producers thought I might be interested in taking over at a later date – the villain of the piece, naturally. So I went along.

Debbie, who had written and directed *Nativity* 1, 2 and 3, works in an improvisational way and I was really interested to see how that worked. As a director and choreographer, I think it's important to know how your contemporaries work, and I wanted to see the outcome of an improvised rehearsal period when it finally opened on stage.

Before curtain up, I met David in the theatre bar for a drink. I was introduced to Debbie and we started chatting.

'It's very brave to improvise a whole show,' I said. 'It must be really difficult.'

'I love it,' she said. 'It's more spontaneous, they can change the words every night, and tell the story in a different way every night, as long as they get from point A to point B.' She talked me through how it worked and said there were certain parts that had to be included and that, as far as she was concerned, it didn't matter how the actors got there, as long as they told those parts of the story. Obviously, the songs had to be learnt because they involved lots of kids.

It was really interesting. When I saw it, I thought, 'Yes, that really worked.' It just felt very true, like it was coming from the actor for real, and there were so many great characters in it. Debbie is a total genius. She's really down to earth and unassuming and we got on well straight away. I was so impressed at how she could go into a rehearsal room without a script, with nothing, and produce such a wonderful show.

While I don't go in with any thought in my head in terms of direction or choreography, I always have a script and an overall opinion of the piece. I know the scenery because that's all pre-planned, but I don't really have any ideas of what I want the actors to do until we get into the play and they start speaking and moving. I like to keep an open mind.

In that way, Debbie and I work in a similar fashion, in that we are spontaneous and on the spot, but at least I always have a working script to go in with. I found the fact that she didn't bizarre and scary, but I liked the idea of it.

Anyway, I really enjoyed the show, the audience loved it but I didn't know whether the part was for me. When the producers rang and asked me if I was interested, I told them the role was a bit small and, without being big-headed, that particular villain part didn't, for me, achieve what I would like to achieve. There wasn't a song that I felt I could sing and the arc of the character wasn't big enough for me, particularly after playing Hannigan.

So, I declined that offer and thought, 'I'll wait and see what happens.' They were talking a year in advance here and I didn't want to commit to anything.

A month later, I got another call from Debbie Isitt.

'Oh, hi, Craig,' she said. 'I'd like to offer you a part in my next movie.'

I nearly dropped the phone. I couldn't believe it.

'That sounds interesting,' I said, trying to conceal my excitement. 'Which movie is that?'

'It's one of the *Nativity* movies, the fourth one in the series, and it's called *Nativity Rocks!*,' she said. 'There's a character I'm writing at the moment that I would love you to play.'

She started going into the character who was to become Emmanuel Cavendish, although she had no name for him at the time.

'This is his background,' she said. 'He was born in Coventry, moved to L.A. He became a Hollywood director and a director of epic, arena productions. But he's a total diva and the villain of the piece.'

Being a director myself, I thought, would make it much easier to play the director and diva she was talking about. Debbie explained that he's not liked but there is redemption so, she said, 'You won't just come out as like the nastiest person on Earth.'

I had never done a movie and I thought this would be brilliant so, of course, I said yes.

They had wanted to film in January but that was going to be impossible for me, because I would be on the *Strictly* tour, so they changed the start date to mid-February, a week after the tour ended, which meant another back-to-back job. As time was tight, all the preliminary work such as the costume fittings, wig fittings, make-up and all of those decisions had to be made during the day, before the *Strictly* shows at Wembley.

First came the costume fitting. The costume designer and his team came into my suite at the Hilton Wembley, where I was staying for the tour, and filled up my entire room with costumes. Then all afternoon I was trying on outfits and thinking, 'Oh my God, I'm in a costume fitting for a movie!'

What was odd was that I still didn't really know my character, as I would if I had read a script. The stylist was saying, 'Are you happy about that?' and I would say, 'I think so, but I don't really know what the character would wear.'

The outfits he brought were outrageously flamboyant, and there were hundreds of them. There were paisley-print tight trousers in black and white teamed with a flamboyant fake-leather, floral-printed biker jacket; a white, ruffled New-Romantic-style shirt and loads of rings (one or two for every finger, including thumbs), all over the top of skin-tight red leather gloves. Another outfit was a sparkly wool jumper with crazy biker-glam Swarovski-crystal jewellery at the neckline and more outrageous rings on every finger, teamed with men's five-inch heeled boots. They totally went to town.

Each time I tried an outfit on I paraded up and down, and then the costume designer took a photo and sent it to the director. When I arrived on set there was a costume pool specifically for me, so that we could choose on the day what Debbie wanted me to wear. In the end, I only wore two outfits out of a hundred.

Tour over, I travelled up to Coventry for filming. I was really nervous on the first day because I didn't know what my character name was, I didn't know who I was, I didn't know what I was doing there. All I knew was that I was a director from L.A., but I had been born in Coventry. I also didn't know that I was filming a big scene on the first day. They keep the shooting structure hidden from the actors. So wardrobe knew, make-up knew, but no one could tell me.

First stop was wardrobe, where they dressed me in various outfits and sent the photo down to Debbie on the set. Then she had to say 'Yes' or 'No, change that to something more floral.' They'd come back to me with a new costume and say, 'You're not wearing that, you're wearing this.'

After that, it was off to make-up where they told me, 'You've got to be over-tanned for this and we need to pluck your eyebrows. This is the wig you're wearing.'

'Oh, okay,' I thought. 'I've got long hair and too dark a tan.' I was trying to piece the character together in my head.

I tried several long wigs of various colours. They weren't sure whether to put my hair in a ponytail or not, so they tried that and no one liked it, then they tried braiding it, but no one liked that either. I liked the idea of having it hanging loose so I could swish it around. Finally, I put another wig on, shook my head upside down, and the photo went down to the set. Debbie said, 'Yes, that's the one,' and so that's the one we went with.

I walked out of make-up a completely different person. I looked into the mirror and got a real shock. I didn't know who I was. I had this ludicrous outfit, long hair, an orange tan and big glasses. The team had achieved the aim of Karl Lagerfeld meets Liberace. I couldn't stop taking pictures of myself in the mirror because I didn't recognize myself at all.

'I wonder how he'd talk,' I said to myself. I had no idea. 'Do I have an American accent? Do I speak like me? Have I become posh and lost the Coventry accent?' In the end I went for posh, or pretending to be posh, because he's a completely up-himself character, totally full of his own piss and wind. Also, as I discovered in time, he hated Coventry and that's why he left, so he would want to lose the accent. The only reason he came back was because he had been offered this big job which was going to put him on the map back in England again and the Arts Council would award him prizes. It was all for his own ego. When I found out about all of this, I thought he would have a posh voice from the south, and that would make him stand out in L.A. Over there he would have lied and said he was from London and he would be affected, like a terrible theatrical queen.

I didn't have much time to decide what I was going to do, because I was thrown straight in. The next thing I knew, I was in the back of a taxi to the set, dressed up in this hideous outfit, with a whole bunch of actors I'd never met before, who were also dressed up in character.

'What character are you playing?' I said to the man next to me, who turned out to be a journalist called Darren Parkin from Coventry, who was doing some acting on the side.

'I'm playing a reporter,' he said. 'I've got to interview this guy who is arriving, I think, from L.A. and he's a big star over there.'

'That sounds like me,' I said. 'I think you're going to be

interviewing me. Do you know what you're going to ask me?'

No,' he said. 'I just know that I'm asking someone called Emmanuel Cavendish questions.'

That was the first time I heard my character's name actually uttered by anyone. I had seen my character name on the screen when I checked into the hotel, because it was used to keep our identities secret, and then again on my trailer door, but hearing it out loud meant it all became a horrible and terrifying reality.

'I think we're going to be working together,' I said. 'Have you been told anything else.'

'No, nothing,' he said.

So, we arrived on set, and I was beside myself with nerves. I've got to be honest, I really was having kittens over the whole thing.

'What if I can't do it?' I kept asking myself. 'What if I get in front of the cameras and I freeze and nothing comes out? What if I fail? I can't fail, it's on celluloid forever. Why am I doing this?'

The answer was that it was exciting, it was a challenge, and I love challenges. As nervous as I was, I was also very excited.

I was relieved to see a few friendly faces on set. There were some actors I knew, auditioning for their roles. Jon Robyns, who played Eddie in *Sister Act*, was there, and so was Helen George from *Call the Midwife*, who I knew, of course, from *Strictly*. Ashley Pollitt, who I'd worked with on *Fiddler on the Roof*, was stage manager and David James Hulston was assisting the director. They had worked with Debbie on *Nativity: The Musical*, and then she took them from that to do the film.

David is usually my assistant but this time I was the silly little actor freaking out, while he had all the power. It was a role reversal and it was so weird because he could tell me what to do, but it was a relief to see him on set that day, when I was in such a petrified state.

As soon as I arrived, Debbie came up to say hello.

'Oh, you look good,' she said. 'That looks great. Like the outfit. Yes, that's all good.'

I was trying to get used to my new long hair, sunglasses I've never worn before, fur coats, Liberace rings, Karl Lagerfeld zhoosh. It was a crazy look, like a fashion icon that's all bad taste.

Then I spotted some Louis Vuitton luggage going around the corner and I thought, 'That must be for me,' and Debbie confirmed it was.

'Your assistant is going to be wheeling it and your assistant's name is Tony.'

Ah, so that's his name.

'Right, here's the situation,' Debbie continued. 'You walk around the corner, you see adoring fans who are all screaming for you. You can smile, maybe wave or something at them and then get to this point. Then cameraman two will pick you up from over there and you walk in a straight line over to them. A reporter is going to ask you a few questions, which you need to answer. Big up the fact that you're doing a *Nativity* rock opera.'

It was the first time I'd heard any of this.

'Okay,' I said, terrified. 'Am I directing it?'

'Yes, you've been asked to direct,' she said. 'You can mention the fact that there are going to be floats and fireworks and you want Coventry to win Christmas Town of the Year.'

So that was it. As soon as she'd finished her explanation, she said, 'Right, are we ready, everyone? Action.'

'Oh my God, she just said "action",' I was thinking. Talk about being thrown in at the deep end!

I walked down to the end of a corridor with about four lifts either side, with my fictional PA heaving all my Louis Vuitton luggage behind me. We were in an office block with real workers and the foyer was dressed to resemble an airport. Every now and then we had to stop filming, as the actual staff needed the lifts and would consistently walk into shot. It was chaotic and quite hilarious. There were hundreds of extras everywhere, camera crews, lighting, desk staff and so on.

I had to face the crowd and make a great speech about everything I loved about Coventry, things I might have hated that I can change, and why I was back in the city. As soon as I started, something clicked and I just went into character. I didn't even know how my character walked until I started down that corridor and I instantly started strutting for some reason. Whatever happened at that minute, I had to keep that character from that moment on.

The whole thing was bizarre. I don't think I breathed through the whole scene because I've got all these people in front of me and reporters asking me questions. My God, it was unbelievable, it was such a trip. The adrenaline rush, the endorphins that were released in my brain – I couldn't wait to do it again. It was amazing.

After the first take, Debbie wanted to do it again and she told me not to say the same thing twice. In the end we did it three times and it was completely different each time.

I did that scene and they said, 'That's a wrap.' I couldn't believe it was over so quickly. I was sent back to my trailer, and told, 'You've got another scene tomorrow.'

'Can I ask what it is?' I said, hopefully.

'No,' came the unequivocal answer.

The next day, we were dressed and made-up and put in the taxi again, still blind to our fate. I was in the same outfit, so I knew it was the same day, and wherever I was going from the airport is where the next thing would take place.

Unlike most films, which work out of sequence, Debbie works chronologically, which helps the actor get their head around the sequence of events. It helps build the character and stops you getting confused and not knowing where the emotional plot should be. If you're improvising that's almost essential, because whatever the characters are saying creates the script along the way. I didn't realize that until towards the end of the movie, when I was bringing up stuff that I had mentioned in that very first scene, the airport arrival. It was the oddest thing. You forget what you have said because you are literally making it up as you go along. It is insane, but every actor is in the same boat and it certainly keeps you on your toes.

So, I rocked up on set and saw a red carpet, with hundreds of people standing and gathering along the ropes, and a waiting limo.

'You're in the limo,' said Debbie. 'Get out of the limo and then you'll give a news interview on the national news, and it is about you returning to Coventry and bringing a really amazing show. So when I call "action", the limo will drive up and then you get out.'

All I could think was, 'How am I going to get out of

the limo?' My hip was killing me, and although I was on painkillers just to be able to get through the day, it was still agony. I was also wearing boots with five-inch heels. I had no time to practise getting out of the car and I was worried I would get stuck or just make a really clumsy exit.

Somehow, though, when the time came, I did this huge développé ballet move out of the limo and managed to pull it off. What a relief.

A reporter came over and started asking me questions. I was addressing the crowd, talking about what I am going to do with the show, then I walked up the red carpet and that is the last of me for that scene. It was great fun.

Another weird thing about the improvised shoot is that you don't know who the rest of the cast is until you share a scene, so a famous face can suddenly appear. On one occasion I was filming a scene where I am auditioning for the show, sitting at a desk with my assistant and judging performances, like on *Britain's Got Talent* but with snarly remarks, and Celia Imrie walked in. I confess I was a bit star-struck. She has been an icon of mine ever since I came to this country. Although I had seen a caravan with her name on it, I didn't know if I would be filming with her, so it came as a huge surprise to meet her like that.

Celia plays a very straight-laced, ambitious headmistress of the school who wants to be in the production I was directing. When they finally get into the show, I have to envision what parts they are going to play within the nativity, and she wanted to be the angel Gabriel.

'Okay, let's try you out at that,' I said. 'But I am thinking a dark, sinister, satanical version of this angel, because it is *Nativity Rocks!*'

Really, it's my intention to destroy the community, egotistically, because I wanted to play all the parts myself and be the big star. I discovered this from Debbie after the audition scene.

'You really want to be in it, but you don't want her to be in it,' she said. 'So do something that makes her not want to be in the nativity to prove that she can't do it, to test her.' So I had Celia Imrie all in black, writhing around on the floor and then coming up through a grave and singing opera.

She did it, like everything she does, brilliantly, and it is hilarious, but fantastic. I would never have imagined I would one day work on a feature film with Celia Imrie. But she was a joy – adorable, friendly and incredibly funny.

Other people that popped up in scenes were Hugh Dennis, Helen George, who had her baby with her in the trailer with a nanny all through the shoot, and Anna Chancellor, 'Duckface' from *Four Weddings and a Funeral*. The first time she came into one of my scenes, she came hurtling around the corner and fell over and slipped on her arse, because there was a little ramp and she tripped. They were filming the whole thing.

She got up, said, 'I'm fine, I'm fine,' then walked straight back in the door and came round the corner again and I had to have a scene with her. She started to berate me for not including the homeless and I had no clue who her character was, so I had to say, 'Who are you?'

It is quite bizarre to meet someone for the first time in a scene and being introduced to their character. As in real life, you have to remember their names and what they do. You react immediately. I love that way of working. I would do it again in a heartbeat.

The whole thing was nerve-wracking but there was one scene I really lost sleep over.

As I left the set one evening, Debbie handed me a song sheet.

'Can you learn this song for tomorrow, because you are going to have to perform it,' she said. 'I am thinking that maybe you should be Herod in the nativity play, so if you can learn this song, we will film that tomorrow.'

That threw me into a panic. I would normally have two or three weeks to learn a song and choreograph it. I was up half the night trying to memorize it. The next morning, I was in rehearsals for the choreography and still trying to learn it. That night I had to perform it, in front of thousands, on the stage at Coventry Cathedral, along with all the kids. It was unbelievable and incredibly frightening, but we pulled it off, and it was a great experience.

After my niece's fairy-tale Tinder romance, I was up for finding my Prince Charming on the dating app. To my surprise, I found I really liked talking to the people on Tinder because it seemed to cast a wider net, in terms of age and background.

Then, while I was on the 2018 *Strictly* tour, I came across a horticulturalist called Jonathan who looked very attractive. The profile picture was a dark-haired, gorgeous-looking lad sitting on a kid's tractor laughing and having fun. That piqued my interest, so I looked at some more photos. In every one, he was laughing or smiling in a natural and unselfconscious way.

On most Tinder pics, people go out of their way to look brooding by pushing their lips forward and pouting. A lot of them are digital makeovers that you can tell are Photoshopped to within an inch of their lives. With filters and doctoring, you can add cheekbones and abs, you can change the colour of your eyes, you can change exactly what you look like. But these photos were real, honest photos that looked like they had captured a moment on camera rather than a manufactured pose that had been Photoshopped to death. It was a refreshing change from all those ghastly doctored photographs.

I thought, 'I wouldn't mind meeting him.' I swiped right and we started talking.

Jonathan lived in Leicester and I was in Nottingham, forty-five minutes away. I only had an hour before I had to go off for my matinee, so I suggested brunch.

'Yes, I'm in,' he replied.

'Let's meet at my hotel at eleven a.m. and we'll have a one-hour brunch before I go to work,' I said. He said he would drive down from Leicester in the morning.

Unfortunately, his car had blown up on the A47 the day before, so he had asked his auntie Janis to drive him to Nottingham and she wasn't impressed.

'You're not really going on a date with that Craig Revel Horwood?' she said. 'He's nasty. He's a horrible, horrible person.' She tried to convince him not to meet me.

Luckily, he liked my pictures, because they were natural and smiley. I didn't use professional or publicity shots and I didn't doctor them. It really was me on Tinder.

But Jonathan is not a *Strictly* fan, so he had no preconceived ideas of me. He's a bookworm and a horticulturist who trained at Kew Gardens, and he doesn't watch many shows on telly. He is very intelligent and he'd rather read a good book, which I love. But he decided to take a chance and come because of my pictures.

Obviously, he googled me after we started talking, as we all do to check each other out, but it didn't seem to put him off. And, luckily for me, his auntie reluctantly agreed to bring him and drop him off at my hotel.

We just wanted to see what one another looked like in the flesh, to chat, and it was bit like a speed date. But as soon as he walked in the door I thought, 'Oh my God, he's absolutely gorgeous.' He looked exactly like the photographs: dark, tousled hair, short beard and a smiling, happy face.

We chatted for the next hour and we got on like a house on fire. There were no nerves or awkwardness. It was perfect, as if we'd known each other for years. I was smitten.

After the date, I went off and did the matinee, wondering when I would be able to see him again. We were on the last leg of the tour and about to head back to London. I finished the tour on the Sunday night at the O2 and I had a holiday booked with my friend Alex Murphy at the Body Holiday resort in St Lucia, because I only had one week before I started filming in Coventry for *Nativity Rocks!*. After months of working seven days a week, day and night, I needed a short break to recharge my batteries. At the time, I don't think I could physically have been any busier.

'The timing is not great,' I told Jonathan. 'I'm going away to St Lucia and my life is pretty crazy at the moment. But I do have one weekend off before I have to go up to film in Coventry.'

I had looked on the map and Coventry is only an hour from Leicester, so I said, 'There would be time to see you while I'm there but, in the meantime, are you brave enough to come to my house for the weekend?'

It was a big leap of faith. We had literally met each other for one hour. Although we had been Facetiming in between, it was still a bit of a bold move and it might not have worked out. We hadn't even kissed, so it was slightly nerve-wracking to say the least.

But he said 'Yes', and he came down to stay at the house. We had a wonderful weekend which ended up being four days, because my filming was delayed by two days and he was able to take an extra couple of days off.

We got on brilliantly and we've been together ever since. In June, he came on a cruise with me and met my brother Trent and the family, and he's coming to Australia with me next year.

It didn't take long for him to introduce me to his mum and dad and his siblings, who were all lovely. Like me, he's got three sisters and a brother, so he understands the complex dynamics of a large family. They invited me on his family holiday and I took my mum, so it's worked out really well.

Having a horticulturist around is quite handy because I have such a big garden, and I'm a terrible gardener. He's already made some beautiful changes around the place and he's a lovely, genuine, gorgeous person so I feel very lucky.

By the end of *Nativity Rocks!* the pain from my hip was unbearable, but fitting the operation into my schedule was never going to be easy. I had signed all the contracts with P&O to do the cruises a year in advance. I also sign contracts for panto five years in advance and I have to make sure I'm fit enough for that every year. Obviously, I also need to be fit for *Strictly*, my top priority.

I finally managed to schedule a break in May.

I went in for X-rays, almost exactly a year after the last ones, and the surgeon, the wonderful Professor Justin Cobb, said, 'This hip is really bad. It's actually worse than the last one. I really don't know how you've been walking.'

'Neither do I,' I said. It was just the motivation of work that had kept me going. I was limping badly, even though I had been unaware of that until people started pointing it out. Press photographers would be asking me why I was limping when I came out of the hotel on tour, so I told everyone I needed another hip operation.

Professor Cobb told me I definitely needed a hip replacement and my first reaction was 'Thank God'. I couldn't have put up with another year of pain and it would have stopped me working. He said he could do it on 1 May. I was delighted, because that gave me exactly three weeks recovery before I needed to get on the ships for the *Strictly* cruise. The only worry was that I had to pick up the first cruise in Gibraltar, so the first question I asked was, 'Can I fly after three weeks?'

'There shouldn't be a problem with that,' he said. 'Depending on recovery.'

To be honest, the ships are a good place to recuperate. Pretty much everyone has had a hip replacement! There are people in wheelchairs or with walking sticks everywhere and they are very well catered for, plus you can go up and down in lifts to every deck. I just have to get to the theatre twice to judge the passengers' *Strictly* and for a Q&A interview, and run a book-signing session, but I can sit down for that.

After that, Trent was coming over so I took a bit more time off to give myself the full recovery time of six weeks.

The hip operation went incredibly well, as it had the first time. After just five days I was back at home and on my way to a full recovery.

For the first six weeks, I had to use the pool for exercises. Because I had known I was going to get my new hip, I had put in a hydrotherapy pool and had the heating put on in the outdoor pool. The alternative was a long trip to the hospital to use the hydrotherapy pool, every single day for a thirty-minute session, and I would much rather do it comfortably at home. Every day I did an hour of exercises in the pool, even if it was pouring with rain. I wanted to make sure I was in peak condition as soon as I could.

There was a lot of pain in the first days and weeks, but that was to be expected. There were also piles of pills to pop every day to manage the pain, prevent blood clotting and so on, and they made me feel a bit tired. But I knew from my previous op that all of this is worth the end result.

Jonathan took two weeks off to look after me, to nurse me while I recovered at home. I couldn't have done it without him.

At first I thought, 'I'm strong. I can do this on my own. I don't need anyone.' But actually I did need him. It wasn't only as an emotional support but also for someone to be there to help me move things about and do normal daily activities which you forget you can't do. You can't bend down, so you have to have a litter-picker, it takes forever to walk up a few steps and it's quite alarming the help that you do need. The hospital asked me if there was someone at home who could help me and I was relieved to be able to say 'Yes'. Jonathan was a godsend.

After Jonathan went home, my old friend Magatha came down to stay and looked after me well. My recovery couldn't have gone better. After three weeks, I was able to fly to Gibraltar for the cruise, and by the time Trent and his family arrived to stay with me, I was almost back to my twirling, whirling best.

With my two new titanium hips I feel like a new man. Thank goodness for the wonders of modern medicine.

CHAPTER 13

Waxing Lyrical

n August 2017, I received the most astounding message from my agent, Gavin. 'Darling,' it read, 'Madame Tussauds want to make a waxwork of you!'

The forwarded email revealed that visitors to the Blackpool attraction had 'overwhelmingly' requested a model of little old me to be added to the collection.

It would, the email explained, require three hours of my time to sit for the team of artists who would create the wax figure at any time that was convenient to me.

'OMG,' I thought. 'What an honour!'

My next thought was, 'Why would they want me?' I felt compelled to immediately open the attachment, which revealed that a waxwork of me had been 'highly requested' by their visitors. Little old me! I couldn't believe it.

It went on to say they would be honoured if I would join their cast of iconic figures in their waxwork museum and, fittingly, my likeness was to stand in the Blackpool museum, close to the Tower Ballroom.

I was fascinated by the explanation that followed of how it

would be done. The letter said the team would take hundreds of measurements and that the waxwork would take twelve weeks to complete. They invited me to a sitting, where they would measure every bit of me, assess my skin tone, eye colour etc., which would take approximately three hours, and promised to reflect my 'personality and depth', which can't be easy in a waxwork. Finally, the letter asked me to launch the work of art in Blackpool, when it was ready to be unleashed on the public, and asked me to keep the whole thing secret until then.

Gobsmacked, shocked, astounded, staggered, flabbergasted, caught totally off balance but utterly delighted – that was my initial reaction to the letter and I couldn't wait to tell the family. They would never in a million years believe it. I had been given the opportunity of being captured in time before any more wrinkles arrive and being immortalized forever by the most famous company in the world. I thought I was dreaming.

I assumed my wax figure would be sitting at the *Strictly* desk with the other judges holding a score paddle, but no. It turned out it was just me on my lonesome. I was beyond excited.

The next letter I received, however, was the 'creative figure brief'. I have to confess it sent me into a slight spin. It asked for thoughts on 'pose, expression, styling, etc'.

It went on to list the various checks and measurements they would take on the day.

- *Head and body measurements and photographs*
- *Colour matching for skin tone, hair and teeth*
- *Head scan*
- *Tooth cast*

- *Hand cast*
- *PR – approx. 15 minutes for an interview and sound bites required. Anything we later release will be sent for your approval.*

It also requested that I needed to change into skin-tight shorts and vest so that 'sculptors can see the contours of the body'. That was the most alarming sentence in the email, as far as I was concerned. Who would ever want sculptors to see the true contours of their body? It all sounded excruciatingly embarrassing, but for a true, life-size replica of me it simply had to be done. I was truly excited. In fact, I couldn't wait to get the wheels in motion and see how it was all created. A date was set, and we were off and racing towards waxwork heaven.

On the day of my first session, I arrived at the London studios feeling a little tentative and nervous, not knowing what to expect. I was met at the door by some of the Madame Tussauds artistic team, who were absolutely delightful, and they took me up to the fourth floor. It all seemed very secretive, like I was in *Charlie and the Chocolate Factory*, entering a world of pure imagination and a place where only special people with a gold winning ticket could gain access. Very few have crossed the threshold and all that have returned eternalized, enshrined and glorified in wax. Immortality was just hours away.

I was introduced to the thirty-strong team, meeting them all individually, then I was made to feel comfortable and it was down to business. Yes, it was time for the dreaded de-robing.

I was asked to go behind the screen and change into light grey Lycra shorts and a skin-tight singlet and to come out when I was ready. It was pretty daunting to walk out in such skimpy gear in front of the massive team that was to sculpt, paint, measure, prod, poke and photograph me and I felt unusually vulnerable and exposed.

Once I had tentatively emerged from behind the screen, I was placed on a high chair and hundreds of black dots were made on my face and neck with a marker pen, then coloured sticky dots were placed over my entire body. Next, I was asked to stand on a revolving plate, like a large Lazy Susan, with millimetre-precision measurements drawn onto the base of it. The team requested that I chose a dance position that would allow visitors to interact with my figure when it was in situ and, not knowing quite what I was in for, I chose to lunge on one leg, with one arm up high and one arm out to the side.

As soon as I was in position, the plate began to turn slowly, through five millimetre revolutions, while intricate and meticulous measurements of my head and body were taken with callipers and crossed referenced to a chart on a table close by. Photos of every part of my head and body were also taken at every five millimetre turn of the dais.

This went on for several hours and was actually quite exhausting. Naturally, I had to stop for short breaks, as my arms and legs were shaking due to holding the position for such a long time. Lactic acid was building up in my muscles due to pointing my foot, holding a straight leg to the side and my supporting leg in a lunge. I was getting a proper workout but it was only on the one side as I couldn't shift my weight or move a muscle. My feet had to be drawn around so they had to be kept in the exact same position all the way through and the whole thing seemed to last an eternity.

After the measuring and photos were done, the skin-tone specialists arrived to take pigmentation measurements, colour matching all my natural skin tones which differ more than you may think on a person's face, neck, hands and body. They even take note of freckles, moles, blemishes and, in fact, all your imperfections, which I may have preferred to gloss over.

Next, the eye specialists arrived to study the many colours of my eyes, lashes, whites of eyes, reactions of my pupils to daylight, etc. They had a whole series of eyes that might match and compared them to my natural eyes, which was quite freaky and, as that had to be done in daylight, the doors of the studio were flung open.

I felt like I was being studied for some bizarre experiment, or being scrutinized in a zoo.

After a fifteen-minute lunch, when they laid on an amazing spread, it was all about the teeth. Size, colour and shape were all scrutinized and recorded and all the time photographs were being taken of every aspect. I also had to have my dentist make up a replica of my teeth in plaster of Paris, to be sent onto them at a later date.

Hair was the next thing and yes, they reproduce every single grey hair mixed in with my natural brown.

It turned out that three hours was a bit of an underestimate. My first session alone took four hours, with further sessions booked for a later date. But it's just incredible how much detail they go into. You can see why it takes a team of thirty on the day to get all the work done and why it takes four hours. The Tussauds team were just fantastic and extremely professional on every level, and they really looked after me. I simply couldn't wait for round two.

Round two arrived, it seemed quite swift, and when I walked in the studio I got a bit of a shock. There before me stood a Craig Revel Horwood effigy in clay. When you look in the mirror you see a reverse image of yourself and never a true image in 3D, the way you're viewed by other people. I found it really strange and quite spooky. I couldn't stop staring at it. The detail in my neck, the back of my head, my ears from behind, the profile, the stark reality of how I'm seen by others was alarming, but at the same time it's your twin and you sort of want to hug it. It had absolutely no colour on it and was just a flat grey mould, but somehow it had personality.

The second session was to refine the detail of the figure and make direct comparisons to the real me. I'd been in *Annie* in the West End at the time and dancing daily, so I'd lost a bit of weight since the first session. They had to shave off some of my jawline as it was more prominent and also take an inch off my belly, which I was positively thrilled about.

As part of the deal I had to supply the clothing from my own wardrobe including a tuxedo, shoes, a watch, shirt, bow tie – the full Monty. At the team's request, I changed into that and put myself back into the dance position beside my alter ego as pictures were taken of both of us together, so they could see how the clothes should fall on the figure. This visit also included the moulding of my hands, which involved sticking my hands and arms into a liquid substance which turned to rubber around them. There was a moment of panic when my arms literally got stuck. I had to wriggle them out by letting air into a small gap I created with a leaning movement of my arm which, in turn, let out an almighty fart, which kept us all amused for ages.

I had one final visit and that was about getting personality and life into the face. To do that, I just had to sit down and talk to the sculptor, so he could study details such as how I move and react when I smile, how my smile lines work and how much white you can see in my eyes.

The final sitting went well, and was certainly more comfortable than the first, and I was then taken on a tour of the studio. It was fascinating. In the body workshop, sculptors were working on around twenty different figures from all around the world, all of them headless. In the next room, all the clay heads were being meticulously crafted down to the most minute detail. The painters' room, where the heads had no eyes or teeth, was like a scene from a horror movie. The next room had a long line-up of disembodied heads, almost finished. There I saw the wax modelled heads of the Queen, Donald Trump, Kylie Minogue, Beyoncé, Brad Pitt, George Clooney and a famous Japanese pop star, all having touch-ups at each artist station. It was like walking into a backstage make-up room at the *Strictly* studio, only the heads had no body. The features were so lifelike, it was uncanny.

The final room was where the waxwork comes together with head, body and costume. So many artists work together to make this one perfect creation and seeing the figures there was like being at the world premiere of a movie. The only thing missing was the banter and the paparazzi. What a privilege to become part of this amazing company of famous names.

The grand unveiling of my waxwork effigy in Blackpool was originally set for August but they completed my figure early, so we were able to move it forward to 2 July 2018. This was a happy coincidence, because my brother Trent and his family were visiting from Australia for the first time in fourteen years, and my mum was also over for her annual visit. We all took a people carrier to Blackpool, took in the Pleasure Beach and all the other quirky things Blackpool has to offer – Kiss Me Quick hats, donkeys, fish and chips, Blackpool rock and so on. The weather couldn't have been more perfect. It was a lovely hot summer weekend, with blue skies and sunshine a-plenty, in stark contrast to the freezing temperatures I have often encountered when *Strictly* hit town in mid-November.

The unveiling was to take place on Monday morning at the most famous ballroom of them all, Blackpool Tower Ballroom. It's familiar territory for me, of course, because we film the show there each year but I never cease to be awestruck by its opulent beauty.

I was asked to arrive early in the morning for colour checks with the figure, to make sure our skin tones still matched. There was an artist at hand to make last-minute changes and it was just as well, because I was much more tanned than I had been in the middle of winter, when I was last seen. The artist hastily but deftly bronzed my figure up to match my tanned face before the press were let in to meet us both.

Walking into Blackpool's Tower Ballroom and seeing my effigy for the first time was spellbinding. It was as if I was in the room doing a show. I was dressed in all my own clothes and shoes in the middle of a routine surrounded by dancing girls with the spotlight on me in the centre of the famous sprung floor of the ballroom. Even my family were taken aback, because none of us expected it to look that real. When I stood in the same position next to the waxwork, it was almost impossible to tell us apart. In fact, you'd probably swear the waxwork was the real CRH, if you had to choose.

The launch went really well, with pyrotechnics and glitter cannons exploding and dancing girls with feather backpacks, then it was onto the six o'clock news, and interviews with papers and magazines. It was all over in a flash, but the beauty of the waxwork figure is that it is now in Madame Tussauds for all to see and interact with. It even speaks when you squeeze my hand, spouting some of my well-known catchphrases like 'dance disaster, darling', 'fab-u-lous', 'a-ma-zing' and some other choice ones that you will have to go to Blackpool to hear for yourselves.

It was a great experience that I'll never forget and what an amazing opportunity. How very lucky I am to have been honoured with such an incredible adventure. Thanks to everyone who requested it, because I had the time of my life.

It's absolutely fitting that my waxwork stands in a popular visitor attraction in Blackpool, the home of ballroom, as *Strictly Come Dancing* has been such a huge part of my life for the last fifteen years.

CHAPTER 14

Royals, Races and Fond Farewells

When I left Australia for a new life in Europe, I was 23 and my baby brother Trent was just 11. As he was growing up, becoming a man, then a husband and father, I was on the other side of the world. My visits to Australia are brief so I would see him for one or two family barbecues every year and never really got the chance to get to know him and his family properly.

But in the lovely hot summer of 2018, Trent, his wife Clare and my nieces Scarlett, 8, and Layla, 6, came to stay for six glorious weeks. At the beginning of June, I bought my first ever child car seats (a minefield for a non-parent like me) and picked them up from the airport. According to Jonathan, I came back with an Australian accent – after talking to my brother for just an hour.

The trip was something of a convalescence for Clare, who had recently been through breast cancer and had to have a mastectomy. There were a lot of complications and she had had a really tough time so I wanted to plan some fun days out and holidays, to take her mind off it.

Luckily, I had been invited to the opening day of Royal Ascot, in the Royal Enclosure, so that was a perfect event to kick-start their stay. But first we had to get kitted out. None of us had the proper top hats and morning suits and, naturally, Clare needed a fabulous hat, so we went shopping in the torrential rain in London to the store of the royal milliner Philip Treacy, who incidentally created Meghan Markle's hat for the same occasion. Clare nearly keeled over at the price of the hats. Some of them were £150,000 and, while beautiful, I drew the line at spending the price of a small house. But I spotted just the thing – an 'architectural headdress' in ivory tones, reflecting 'transparency and floral romance with the illusion of height'.

'Look, this one's fabulous,' I said.

Swooning at the price tag, Clare said, 'No, we'll order something small.'

'Darling,' I said, 'you're going to be competing with the Queen, you're going to be competing with Meghan Markle. You're going to be competing with Eugenie and Beatrice. If you're in the Royal Enclosure you can't have the same hat as everyone else. It simply has to be a one-off.'

I also bought Jonathan and Trent morning suits, which have to be worn with the proper socks, the proper shoes and, of course, a top hat. It was adding up to a small fortune. Gieves and Hawkes of Savile Row offered to dress me, which was a saving, and I went into their glamourous shop for fittings. It all served as a really exciting build-up to the event.

On the day of the opening, we got a make-up artist and hair stylist for Clare, and then the hat went on and she couldn't fit inside the limo. She had to travel with her head to the side all the way to Ascot. It was hilarious. We were all a bit nervous, especially Trent and Clare, because they'd never been to anything like this before.

It turned out I was right about the hat because ALL the Royals turned up, which is not always the case. We were inches away from the Queen, Prince Philip, Prince Charles, Camilla, Prince Harry, Meghan and Princess Eugenie.

As I have met Camilla so many times through our work with the National Osteoporosis Society, I thought I'd say 'hello'. She was standing with the Queen and Prince Philip so I waltzed over to her purposefully. But as I got closer and closer the armed security guards started standing up and coming to attention, positioning themselves around the Queen. It was quite intimidating and they must have wondered what I was up to, but they let me past and I said, 'Hello, darling, it's lovely to be in here. We're loving every minute.' Camilla asked if it was my first time in the Royal Enclosure and we had a nice little chat.

Trent and Clare could not believe they were so close to the Royals. Trent is a drummer in a heavy metal band so he's more used to swigging beer than champagne and there we were, dressed to the nines and mixing with the upper class, sharing a beautiful luncheon with the Queen. We were even invited into the parade ring where they award the prizes and I was asked to hand out a trophy so I was up on the podium immediately after Harry and Meghan.

One of the other guests of honour was the Honourable Alexander Downer, a former Australian politician and diplomat who was leader of the Liberal Party from 1994 to 1995, and Minister for Foreign Affairs from 1996 to 2007, and later the High Commissioner to the United Kingdom. I had no idea who he was but he was a big celebrity to Trent and Clare, so they got chatting to him, which bowled them over. The races were enthralling to watch but I'm not much of a gambler so I only put a fiver on each one; I won a couple and doubled my money.

At the trackside, I was asked to do a little TV interview and my mum, back at home in Australia, was watching. She told me later she was saying to herself, 'Look at that Sheila in the background with that huge hat on! Who does she think she is?' Of course it was Clare!

As mine was the penultimate presentation, and one doesn't want to be sozzled in front of the Queen, I avoided the champagne until I'd finished, then I downed a couple of glasses before we got in the taxi, laughing and screaming in very high spirits indeed. It was a beautiful and memorable day which ended with the crowds singing *Jerusalem* and *Land of Hope and Glory*. It was all so quintessentially British and Clare had a ball. Most importantly, she carried off the Treacy style with her natural elegance and poise. I was so glad I bought her that hat.

We had wonderful weather all the time they were with me, but I was having a new conservatory built so the house was a bit of a building site. Luckily for Layla and Scarlett, we were still using the pool, but all the tiles around it had to come up so it was surrounded by mud and we were walking on planks to get to it, which wasn't ideal.

Trent's visit also came just a few weeks after the hip operation and I had recovered well but I was facing a new challenge – the nightmare of coming off the painkillers. I had been on strong painkillers for years, in order for me to continue working, and they are dangerously addictive drugs. Although they had been a necessity for me I knew that, once my hip was healed, I had to get myself off them and it wasn't going to be easy.

The surgeon prescribed a course of painkillers after the operation but once those were finished I decided to go cold turkey. I knew that was the only way to stop myself from taking them again, but I wasn't expecting the severity of the withdrawal symptoms. It was two weeks of absolute hell. I had night sweats, I was constantly shaking, I felt nauseous and generally ill all day. I was tired and antisocial and I'd have to take myself off to bed at 9 o'clock at night. Without painkillers I couldn't have done the shows I loved, including *Annie* and the pantos, but they took their toll. I'm so glad my shiny new hip means I can kick them to the kerb for good.

The weekend Trent and the family arrived there was the annual Country Show on at Highclere Castle – where Downton Abbey was filmed – with kids' rides, stalls, games, burgers and hotdogs and so on. The girls loved it. All day, members of the public were coming up to me and saying 'hello' and after a while, Layla said, 'Wow! Uncle Craig, you have a LOT of friends here!'

Because I'm not famous in Australia, they had no idea what I did for a living. But they soon got used to the fact that everyone knew me from the telly when we went on a two week Mediterranean cruise on the *Britannia* – with 3,000 *Strictly* fans on board. There were plenty of people wanting to come and chat then.

After the cruise they had a week in London, and then they left on 3 July so we celebrated Independence Day early with a massive fireworks party. I had some professional fireworks left over from my annual New Year's Eve party because it had been raining and a lot of the wicks had got wet. So when I told them we were having fireworks, they imagined shop-bought garden bangers and whizzers but these went off like the display on the Thames and lasted about 20 minutes so they were amazed. We all sat round the fire pit and had a brilliant time.

My mum came over for their last week and stayed for six weeks. Mum's 76 now and you never know when she's going to be able to make it again so it's really important I take the opportunity and see as much of my family as I can.

While Mum was here I went on my first holiday with Jonathan's family. Every year, the family hire two big eight- to ten-berth boats and sail the Norfolk Broads and Jonathan suggested I squeezed on to one of those. But the party already consisted of his whole family, sixteen of them including loads of kids, plus two dogs, and because Mum was coming I thought we'd better get a separate boat.

I picked a gorgeous luxury cruiser and although I had never sailed one before, we had a quick practice session going up and down the canal, spinning around, going backwards and so on and then they let us loose with it. Jonathan's granny June, who's 86, got on so well with Mum that she soon decided to join me, Jonathan and Mum on our 'yacht' and she was great fun.

During the day, we sailed up the Broads and in the evening we moored up and went to pubs on the shore, but we slept on the boat, which was a new experience for me. The summer of 2018 was one of the hottest I can remember and the boat had no air conditioning. Plus, there was a glass roof, so the lounge area, where we often congregated, was stifling, and sleeping in the boiling-hot cabins was difficult. But the four of us had hilarious nights on board, playing cards, eating, drinking, singing with my mum, a very loud soprano, reaching all the top notes in 'Never Enough', from *The Greatest Showman*, and screeching at the top of her voice.

One evening, we had sailed for about five hours into Norfolk but we mistimed the tide and were almost scuppered by a low bridge. Jonathan and I, who were steering on the top deck, had to lie flat on our backs and we literally went under with an inch to spare. It was ridiculous. That'll teach me to check the tide times – we could have been wedged under there for hours.

Jonathan's gran doesn't drink much and this was the first time she had supped champagne in the morning. I was showing off a bit and serving cocktails on the deck as everyone was sailing past, so June was happily guzzling bubbly in the sun. The trouble was she then had to negotiate all the incredibly steep stairs on the boat. Thankfully, with a bit of help, she managed to escape injury.

After five days on the Broads, the boat was so hot I couldn't bear it, so when we got to Norwich I said, 'Right, ladies, I've booked us all into an air-conditioned hotel.' They had a two-bedroom suite with a king-size bed each and, after the tiny bedrooms in the boat, it was pure luxury spending a night in an air-conditioned room. They really appreciated it.

Despite the heat, it was a wonderful holiday and a real chance to get to know Jonathan's extended family. They are all great fun to be around.

Summer over, it was back to *Strictly* and the 2018 season was another corker. Stacey Dooley really surprised me because she wasn't a natural, but by the final she was incredible to watch.

It took her the whole week of training to get comfortable with the routine but then she came out and produced some amazing dances. She deserved to win. Ashley Robert and Faye Tozer were better dancers, which was reflected in the judges' scores, but Stacey made the most improvement and it was down to the public vote in the final, as it should be.

Stacey's dance partner Kevin Clifton was disappointed that I didn't love their show dance. I told him it was too 'bitty' and scored him an eight, but it was down to personal taste. It didn't stop them winning. There are no hard feelings though. It's just my opinion and, as always, I believe I am fair. I was actually delighted to see Kevin win the trophy, after so many times in the final, and he is such a talented choreographer.

Our other finalist, Joe Sugg, was fantastic. He and Diane worked really well together and she gave him some really cool choreography. He really pulled it together in the end. It was good to include a contestant who's known for being an internet sensation, because it brings in a whole new audience and we are living in a digital world, which we have to embrace. You don't have to be an actor or singer to be famous anymore. Bloggers and vloggers tell real-life stories about themselves and the world they live in and millions are gripped by that, so Joe brought a whole new audience to *Strictly*.

Series 16 of *Strictly* was one of the best ever. It resulted in plenty of success stories with people going on to star in West End shows or getting TV progammes. For me, as always, the series was about the hard work and achievements of the contestants and the fabulous dancing.

*

At the tail end of *Strictly*, as usual, I was back in panto. This time, producer Michael Harrison from the panto company Qdos asked me to do *Cinderella*.

'I'm a bit old for Cinderella, darling,' I said. Michael Harrison laughed and said, 'No, it's the wicked stepmother.'

The previous year, when I reprised the role of the Wicked Queen in *Snow White*, the Chuckle Brothers had been my co-stars and in the interim, sadly, Barry had died. Qdos thought *Cinderella* would work as a way of establishing Paul as a single artist, and they wanted him to play my husband. I was thrilled because we had formed such a great bond in Southampton the year before.

Of course, the first time I saw him, before rehearsals started, was a really emotional moment. I just opened my arms and gave Paul a really big hug and simply whispered in his ear, 'I'll miss him.' Rehearsals were sad too, because Paul was doing similar skits to those he did with his brother, but with another actor, Phil Butler, who played Buttons. It was really difficult and we all shed a tear over that but then we pulled together and said, 'Let's do this for Barry.'

It was a fitting tribute because even though another actor was doing the set skits, you remembered Barry doing them so it was bittersweet. Paul bravely held it together which was particularly difficult on the final night, when emotions run high. But every night he thanked his brother and produced a picture of him, and every night we remembered him.

If I needed proof that my two hip operations were the best thing I've ever done in my life, *Cinderella* was it. This was the first time I'd danced on the stage without pain for years and it felt unbelievable. It was incredibly liberating not having to take a super-strong painkiller just to get through the show and it meant I could dance much better. I get aches and pains like any dancer from sore muscles but the lack of pain in my hips is a miracle. It's incredible surgery.

This version of *Cinderella* had been in the West End the year before, so the sets were incredible, the dancers were amazing and the cast was extraordinary. I had the greatest time. I loved the character – Dame Demonica Hardup – because she could look like a frump and be a bit lumpy and bumpy so I didn't have to starve myself for the whole panto season to fit into body-hugging costumes. There were some wonderful tunes, like 'Fabulous Baby' from *Sister Act*, which of course I was familiar with, and I also got to sing 'I Will Survive' – one of my gay anthems. It was a refreshing change to have a stage family – a husband and two daughters. Playing the Wicked Queen can be quite lonely, as you are often out there by yourself, but this meant I had more people to bounce off and we had a lot of giggles. It was a sell-out season and this Christmas, 2019, I'm back as the Wicked Queen in Manchester. I cannot wait.

As New Year comes in the middle of panto run, and many of the cast can't get home for the short break of one evening and one day, I always have a New Year's Eve party for them. I had a big fireworks night and pool party which went on until 6am and the following day I had a New Year's Day 'drag' lunch for the whole company. Just before the meal, when everyone was milling around drinking champagne, I made an announcement.

'It's time, darlings,' I said. 'I'm about to serve lunch so you all need to go up to the top floor, into the drag wardrobe, put something on and come down as a different character.'

So, while I set the two big tables in the dining room

and kitchen and saw to the huge lasagnes I had cooked, everyone was upstairs screaming with delight at my huge range of costumes and trying on all my wigs. It's classic photo opportunity time because one by one these fabulous characters parade down the central staircase in whatever they've put on. I didn't recognise most people. My driver Stuart was squeezed into a blue gown and Paul Chuckle came down in my white wedding dress.

After lunch we had a big photograph out in front of the house, and then we played games and put music on and everyone was dancing in 6-inch stilettos, dresses and crazy wigs. It mixes it up a bit. Everyone's character changes and people have more fun. My friend Clifford was a huge fan of the Chuckle Brothers and he spent about two hours bending the wedding dress-clad Paul's ear – while dressed in a blue Lady Gaga G-string!

The New Year, as always, brought the *Strictly* live tour which was spectacular. I had been working on the new set, the group dance numbers and the feel of the show, since August, as I do every year, because I want to try to top what we did the year before. But of course I don't know which celebrities will be dancing and I don't have any hand in choosing them myself, which is important for my impartiality on the show.

The 2019 celebs were the four finalists – Stacey, Ashley, Faye and Joe – plus popular favourite Lauren Steadman, Dr Ranj Singh and cricketer Graeme Swann. It was a truly fun and fabulous company where we all got on so well, with no big egos to deal with. Everyone just got on with the job at hand and had a great time doing it.

It was also Shirley's first year on tour, so we had all four judges for the first time ever. That was a great bonding experience. On the TV show, you're in and out and then you don't see each other for another week. In the meantime, I'm in panto, Darcey is busy with all her charity events and Bruno is back and forth to LA so, apart from the odd dance event where I see Darcey, we never meet up.

Having the two ladies on tour meant I could feature them in a dance routine, which included all four of us. Darcey did a ballet-pop mash-up routine to 'Yes Sir, I Can Boogie', then Bruno and I did a routine to 'Dancing Queen' (naturally) and Shirley ended by showing off her world-champion Latin American moves to 'Boogie Wonderland'. The audience went wild every night.

Shirley loved doing the tour and, because we were living in each other's pockets, I got to know her a lot better. It helps to forge a special comradeship.

My annual trip to Australia, after the tour, had a special significance in 2019. A few months earlier, on 17 October 2018, I had received a text message about my grandmother Phonse from my cousin Logan.

It read: '*I just wanted to let you know that [Phonse] started a morphine pump today to make her more comfortable so it will only be a short time before she passes away. She is very peaceful and mostly just sleeping. Much love to you. Loges x*'

We were hoping Phonse was going to make it to her 102nd birthday on 5 February because she was incredibly lively and still had all her faculties. But in October she suddenly became ill and went downhill rapidly.

Two days after the first text, at 3.09 a.m. on Friday 19 October, I received another message from Logan.

It read: *'I am sad to bring you the news that Phonse has passed away this morning. She slipped away very quietly and Mum (Jules) and Aunty Lorraine were with her.'* He added, *'She thought the world of you,'* which meant a lot.

I was due to fly out to Australia in mid-February and had planned to go to Perth to see Phonse, so I was deeply saddened that she had gone. But she had lived an amazingly wonderful life and made it to 101, which isn't bad.

Sadly, I couldn't make the funeral due to work commitments but by all accounts it was a wonderful send-off. Logan wrote: *'It was the most amazing tribute to Phonse. Her funeral was a beautiful occasion and a real celebration of an extraordinary life. You would have been proud of our family and especially Sue, who spoke for the Horwoods so well. You were deeply missed today, we would have loved to have you here but you can know that our grandmother was laid to rest with dignity and love.'* Logan's messages were a real comfort.

When I did finally get to Perth, I went to see her grave, which is next to my grandfather Revel Campbell Horwood's plot. Phonse's headstone had only been put in that week and I was among the first to see it, with Logan, so I paid my respects and said goodbye to her there.

Phonse was an amazing woman and a real powerhouse in the family; a solid matriarch who was just full of love. She was the one who taught me to dry myself in her own unique way when I was a little kid. She said, 'You start with your arms and your legs. Your heart is the last thing you dry because it's the warmest part of you.' Isn't that sweet? I still dry myself that way when I get out of the shower.

Phonse was a wonderful cook, famous in my family for her fishcakes, which she made out of redfin perch, because that's all we could get when I was growing up in Ballarat. Redfin are notoriously bony so she painstakingly sifted through the flesh to make sure there were no bones in them and the result was beautiful.

One of my fondest memories was a lovely time that we spent together, on Mother's Day in Australia, 2009, going through her recipes, writing them all down and practising them together. I still have all her recipes, which I hope to publish one day, and I still cook the dishes she taught me.

In my adult life, I didn't get to see as much of Phonse as I would have liked because she lived in Perth and she never came to the UK. Even if I was in Australia, it was quite a journey to get to her because Perth is a four-and-a-half-hour flight from anywhere else in the country. It's the most isolated city in the world in that it's the furthest away from any other city of comparable size, but it's beautiful.

Phonse's daughters – my Auntie Jules and Auntie Raine – lived with her and looked after her right until the end. When I went to see them this year I felt that her death had left a massive hole in their lives. They are so used to her being around and she was still very sharp, as anyone who saw my *Who Do You Think You Are?* will know. She had an amazing life, was full of great stories and her memory was fantastic. I wish she'd written a book.

That year my trip to Australia was considerably extended, because I landed myself a ten-week job on the Australian version of *Strictly*. A few months earlier, I heard that

Channel 10 were reviving *Dancing With The Stars,* which had previously run on Channel 7 but had been axed four years ago. I said to one of the *Strictly* producers that it would be great to judge that while I was over visiting family and, lo and behold, an offer came through.

The only snag was that the date was then fixed for mid-February and I was on the *Strictly* tour until the 10th. In the end, I had one day to pack and I had to supply my own costumes so I took twenty of my 'TV suits' and all my sparkly shoes for the ten-week series. I had so many cases the airline charged me £2,500 each way – £50 a kilo – in excess baggage. I felt like Victoria Beckham! I arrived on Valentine's Day and literally started work as soon as I landed, turning up at rehearsals with all my luggage in tow.

The Australian *DWTS* is very glitzy and showy, like the US version, but they were forced to add a dance-off halfway through. For the first few shows, good dancers were being eliminated because everyone was voting for the cricketer Curtly Ambrose and Jett Kenny, the surfer son of Olympic athletes Grant Kenny and Lisa Curry, who are very famous in Australia. Jett is stunning but was quite wooden on the dance floor and Curtly was about 6ft 8in and couldn't dance at all – and he was getting through. After week four, when Holly Valance's sister Olympia was knocked out, despite being top of the leader board, they changed the format so the judges had the final say, as we do in the UK.

My fellow judges were Tristan McManus, who was a *Strictly* pro on seasons 12 and 13, and Sharna Burgess, the professional who had just won *Dancing With The Stars* in the US with celeb partner Bobby Bones. They both know what they're talking about but it was the first time they'd ever judged and they were quite nervous at the start.

Four weeks into the show, the judges had to do their own dance with a couple of contestants – which is then judged. I chose a routine to 'Easy Street' from *Annie*, with me playing Miss Hannigan, but I hadn't factored in the quick change. It meant I had seven minutes to go from the desk and get into full drag – three minutes for make-up, two minutes for hair, one minute to get dressed and a minute to get into place.

The other two judges were joined by Steve Irwin's daughter Bindi, who won *DWTS* in the US in 2015, and they gave me scores of 9, 9, 10 – which I'll take any day. But then I had to race off and get changed and I literally had three minutes to get out of drag and back into my suit. In the end, I had no time to get my trousers or shoes on, so I came out with my shirt, tie and jacket on the top half but still wearing a pair of heeled Latin shoes, my suspenders, and lingerie on the bottom. I was sitting behind the desk half Hannigan, half Horwood and the only people privy to it were the studio audience and my fellow judges. They had a hard time keeping a straight face.

The dance actually did me a huge favour because the Australian public hated me at first. They didn't like my demeanour and they didn't get my sense of humour. People were tweeting, 'Why have we got him? He's nasty,' and, 'Send him back to the UK'. I was getting so much abuse online that British *Strictly* fans came to my rescue, wading in on Twitter and saying, 'You'll get used to Craig, that's his sense of humour.' Even my family were up in arms and defending me. But after the Hannigan routine, viewers began to see my comedy side and started enjoying me in the show a lot more.

The TV chef Miguel Maestre was the first contestant voted out. I told him he looked like he'd just come out of a double hip replacement (and I should know). We were on a TV show together the following week and he ignored me, which I thought was strange, because he was normally smiley and friendly. When we met again at the final, I told him, 'Look, I criticize. That's what I'm there for. I'm not there to love, nurture and embrace.' The professional dancers were sticking up for me, saying, 'It's just a show.' Going out first is always difficult and he was actually good to watch because he had a lot of energy.

The second elimination was the wonderful Denise Scott, the funniest Australian comedian I've seen for a long time. I compared her to the 'Hunchback of Notre Dame' and gave her a '1' because of her terrible posture but she took it all in good humour. A few weeks into the run Grant Denyer, who co-presents the show with Amanda Keller, put his back out and had to take three weeks off, so Denise took over. She came on and said, 'It just proves you can be compared to the "Hunchback", score a one and get eliminated and two weeks later you're co-hosting the damn show. The message is, hang on to your dreams, kids!' She was a joy.

Drag queen and *Big Brother* winner Courtney Act was also on the show and was brilliant. I looked forward to seeing her dance every week but in week three she blew our socks off. The theme was 'My most memorable year' and she performed an incredible tango where she started off as Courtney, grappling with gender fluidity, and then ripped off her wig, unravelled her dress and became a (near) naked Shane Jenek. It was such a powerful piece of choreography by Joshua Keefe and it moved the nation. On another occasion she danced a tango/foxtrot as Shane Jenek and I thought it was really brave of Channel 10 and *Dancing With The Stars* to include a same sex couple. It worked really well and was really interesting to watch.

The final was between Courtney, the actor Samuel Johnson and Constance Hall, the 'mummy blogger'. In her blog, Constance is about the furthest from a *Strictly* contestant as you can be. She is very down to earth and makes a virtue of showing the honest face of motherhood and bringing up seven kids. So it was quite extraordinary for her to even commit to it but she did really well.

All three of them were good enough to win but as a judge I would say it should have been Courtney, who actually came second. Samuel Johnson, who won, is a fantastic actor so his dances were entertaining but he wasn't a technical dancer like Courtney, who was the most gifted of the three finalists. But Sam's win was very emotional because in Australia they are dancing for their charities – which gives it a different spin. In Samuel's case, he had set up a charity called Love Your Sister, in honour of his sister Connie, who died of cancer at 40. He had vowed not to act again until he hit a target of $1.5 million and he had already unicycled round Australia to raise money, so I think a lot of people wanted him to win as much money as he could for the cause.

Jonathan came with me for all ten weeks because, for a gardener, winter is a quiet time. All the family popped up to see the show at various times, with Sue acting as my PA and booking flights, tickets and accommodation for all of us. As I was only working on Mondays, I had six days off a week, so we had time to travel all over Australia. We had a wonderful trip to Tasmania, took the family to Hamilton Island, went to Perth to see family and pay my respects to Phonse and then went down to Margaret River, near Perth.

By the time we flew down under, Jonathan had been living with me for three months. The romance had been going well and he had been devoting more and more time to my garden, only doing two days a week in his old job in Leicester. But managing the sprawling estate in Hampshire is a full-time job and Jonathan was the perfect person to fill that role so, in November, he moved in.

The transition went incredibly smoothly. No complications, no dramas. Admittedly, when he started unpacking, he was bemused by the amount of clothing I have in my walk-in wardrobe. I have the telly stuff, the stage stuff, the casual stuff – there's a lot to house. I tried to move some clothes out but it wasn't enough. So Jonathan has now moved all his stuff into another room, which is so much better, and I agreed to have a spring clean when we got back from Australia. To be honest, I was running out of space myself but I had a brutal clear-out and I'm giving fifty suits to charity.

The trouble with TV is that you can only really wear something once, which is a shame. I try to recycle as much as I can and we do at the BBC, because mostly I wear a suit from ASOS or M&S. They're not all Pierre Cardin and Versace! But it will be good to see the more flamboyant ones on someone else's back.

As well as culling my wardrobe, the pair of us have been working on plans for our own vineyard. It won't be ready for six years and the only grapes we can grow are champagne grapes, so we're hoping to have a working vineyard which will create a beautiful sparkling wine. I love British wine and there are some in Hampshire that have already won gold medals. It might also save me a fortune in champagne!

Hopefully the first glass will be ready for my 60th birthday party, in 2025.

Just before I left Australia, Darcey was making headlines having decided to leave the *Strictly* judging panel. I have to admit I had an inkling that she was thinking about leaving when we finished the tour. There was something in the air that suggested this would be her last year. It was nothing specific but I remember her saying, 'I've had seven wonderful years on the show and it's been great.' It was almost like on the tour she was wrapping things up as well, so as much as it was a shock, I was half-expecting it.

I sent Darcey a text saying, 'When I get back, we'll go out for a lovely lunch and a good old natter.' I'd like to continue working with her in some way because I think she's fantastic so I will continue to see as much of her as possible.

In the meantime, I'll miss her sitting next to me on the panel. I'll miss her fun side. She was like a child on the set, always happy, always having a giggle and fun to be around. She was an ally. As much as we'd disagree and she might smack me with her paddle, I'll miss that look of disgust at my scores and the fact that we always had a laugh.

Darcey created that wonderful sense of company fun. She was always great with the dancers and was always down to earth. It felt like we were in a ballet company on tour together – which meant all my dreams had finally come true, even though I wasn't dancing with her. When I walk into work this year, I'm definitely going to miss seeing her smiling face.

The reports of her leaving often read like obituaries, like she was dead. Darlings, she's not dead, she's just left the show and wants to move on to different things. I say 'good on her'. Seven years is a good stretch and she's going out on a high. She has a lot of charity work and patronage and there are a lot of things she does in the ballet world that she wants to devote more time to.

Although I joke about my 'Saturday job', *Strictly* takes up a lot of time away from the TV show itself, with interviews and other commitments, so I completely understand. But I am still loving every minute and have no plans to lay down my paddles just yet.

Strictly has opened so many doors for me and I will be forever grateful to the programme and its many devoted viewers for that. I still adore making the show every year, as well as all the other opportunities it brings, and long may it continue.

Right now I have one word for my life. Three syllables. *Fab-u-lous*!

Acknowledgements

My heartfelt thanks go the following people for helping to make this book possible.

Alison Maloney, for her delicious 'ghosting' skills, endless wonderful meetings over a glass or two of savvy B at various glamorous locations around London and at my country retreat over the very hot summer of 2018.

Susan Lee Mason, my incredibly talented older and wiser sister who provided additional material and did some wicked editing for me.

My mum, for always being honest with me and her love.

My family for putting up with me and their unconditional love and support.

My adorable partner Jonathan.

My incredible friends and personal confidants that have helped me through the bad times and provided much needed support and entertainment throughout my life.

All my gorgeous *Strictly* 'family', for without whom, none of this would be possible.

The BBC for continuing my employment.

All my wonderful and generous theatre 'family' whom I respect not only for their obligations to their talents, but their amazing loyalty, devotion and commitment to the performing arts.

Michael O'Mara books for having faith in me, Louise Dixon and Gabby Nemeth for their editing skills and everyone in their extremely talented team that helped put the whole book together, from the lawyer to the typesetter.

All the valiant, fearless and courageous celebrities I've criticised over the years.

The press for being kind this year.

My heartfelt thanks to the talented people below who performed at my 50th birthday parties:

The UK band and cabaret at Café de Paris:

DJs:
Daniel McLeod – DJ
Nick Meier – DJ

Starstruck:
Rietta Austin – Vocalist and MD
Verna Francis – Vocalist
Melone M'Kenzy – Vocalist
Odette Adams – Vocalist
Tee Green – Vocalist
Kevin Leo – Vocalist
Shaun Anthony – Vocalist
Andy McSkimming – Vocalist
Robert 'Skins' Anderson – Percussion
Tom Walker – Guitar
Winston Blissett – Bass
Carl Hudson – Keyboards
Simon Bates – Saxophone
Henry Collins – Trumpet
Julian Chambers – Drums

Cabaret:
Rietta Austin – Vocalist/Choreographer
Alison Jiear – Vocalist
Marcos White – Dancer
Myles Brown – Dancer
Hot Gussett – Cabaret Show
Val Kelly – Photography

The Australian band at Fort Denison:

The Rietta Austin Band:
Rietta Austin – Vocalist
Barbara Griffin – Keyboards and vocals
Matt Roberts – Guitar and vocals
Chris Frazier – Bass
Greg Ohlback – Drums
Fiona Leigh Jones – Percussion and vocals

Last but certainly not least, thank you to the amazing fans who put me where I am today.

Picture Credits

Plate section 1:
The cast dancing © BBC
The judges © BBC
Bruce Forsyth and Tess Daly © BBC
Judy Murray and Anton du Beke © BBC
Will Young and Karen Clifton © BBC
Class of 2016 © BBC
2016 finalists © BBC
Craig and Bruno Tonioli in Halloween Week: The Sun/ News Licensing
Sister Act poster: Artwork and Design: Meltdown; Photography: Jay Brooks
Annie cast © Annie Tour (UK) Ltd. Photograph of CRH and *Annie* company by Hugo Glendinning.
Craig's Madame Tussauds waxwork: Anthony Devlin/ Getty Images

All other pictures courtesy of Craig Revel Horwood and reproduced with his kind permission.

Index